ReConnecting Worship

Where Tradition
and
Innovation Converge

Rob Weber

with

Stacy Hood

Abingdon Press
Nashville

RECONNECTING WORSHIP:
WHERE TRADITION and INNOVATION CONVERGE

Copyright © 2004 Rob Weber

This book is printed on acid-free, recycled paper.

Library of Congress Cataloging-in-Publication Data

Weber, Rob, 1960-
  Reconnecting worship : where tradition and innovation converge / Rob Weber with Stacy Hood.
    p. cm.
  ISBN 0-687-06393-0
  1. Public worship. I. Hood, Stacy. II. Title.

BV15.W425 2004
264—dc22   2004016677

ISBN 0-687-34021-7 Kit
ISBN 0-687-06393-0 Book only

Scripture quotations, unless otherwise noted, are from the New Revised Standard Version of the Bible, copyright © 1989 by the Division of Christian Education of the National Council of Churches of Christ in the United States of America. Used by permission.

Photo credits: All photos are from Getty Images©. Chalice, by Harnett/Hanzon, p. 8; Trapped, by Romy Ragan, p. 8; Symbols of Christianity, by Stephanie Dalton Cowan, p. 28, 174; Corridor with Open Door, by Lisa Zador, p. 44; Sun, Moon, Stars, Night, and Day, by Harnett/Hanzon, p. 64; Dancing Figure in Hoop, by Harnett/Hanzon, p. 84; Vegetable Soup Pot, by Tess Stone, p. 104 Bouillabaisse, by Tess Stone, p. 122; Chef Stirring Sauce, by Tess Stone, p. 143, 164.

04 05 06 07 08 09 10 11 12 13—10 9 8 7 6 5 4 3 2 1

MANUFACTURED IN THE UNITED STATES OF AMERICA

Contents

Googling the Gospel

I operate with two controlling images for "tradition." One is a professional one, the other a more personal one. My more professional image for "tradition" is that of a treasure chest filled with the "family jewels." In this huge jewelry box are rites and rituals, doctrines and creeds, saints and stories, gestures and icons that have been passed down to us by our ancestors. When we reach into the box and pull out its contents, we should feel free to mix and match what is there, to arrange them in new settings, to handle and wear them in creative ways. But we should never feel free to throw any of them away. Or, even worse, we should never feel free to abandon the gem-studded path walked by our ancestors.

My more personal "image statement" for my own ministry is that of a dumpster-diver. I am a historian-futurist just crazy enough to dive into the dumpster bin of history and get myself dirty retrieving those "gems" we have tossed away across 2000 years of forgetting. It may take some cleaning up and convincing that these are indeed "gems" that we trash at our peril. What keeps me going is the increasing awareness that the more precious the gem, the more precarious its place in the jewelry box.

In this wonderful book by Rob Weber and Stacy Hood, there is a keen sense that "tradition" does not mean going backward, but not wanting to go forward without all the riches and resources available. They understand the difference between innovation that has been merely tinctured by tradition and innovation that has arisen from and been anointed in the tradition. Relevancy has too often equated with "recency." And while the authors are aware that what is understood as "tradition" changes fast, they are also able to discern what is a hodgepodge of nostalgia and self-parody and what is our generation's, our culture's authentic and lasting deposits to the treasure chest.

This book's usefulness far exceeds its number of pages. You will use it with the gospel in one hand and Google in the other.

Leonard Sweet
E. Stanley Jones Professor of Evangelism; Drew Theological School
Distinguished Visiting Professor; George Fox University

A Broken Chalice

She was weeping when she arrived at the front door of my house. She held in her hands a paper bag. I couldn't understand what she was saying through her sobs. I brought her inside and helped her sit down on the couch. "I'm sorry . . . I'm sorry . . . I'm sorry . . ." she said. "What happened? What's the matter?" I asked as I tried to comfort her. It was then that she reached into the bag and brought out the pottery chalice that had been given to me for ordination. It was broken. She had been cleaning the altar and tending to the elements when she accidentally dropped the chalice. She was horrified. Of course I would have preferred that the chalice not have been broken, but my concern was not for the pieces of dried clay, but rather for the hurt in the living heart of this woman with whom I had shared four years of life; studying the Bible every Wednesday morning for a year, worshiping together, and holding her hands as her husband died of cancer. Now, in my living room, holding those same trembling hands again, we prayed. The relationship was far more important than the chalice. By the time she was ready to leave, we had hugged, shared how much we loved each other, and laughed at the children and the squirrels playing in the front yard.

There was something deep going on that Sunday afternoon. It was not really about a piece of pottery. It was about something much deeper and much more complex. Her act of preparing for communion and tending to the elements after the service was an embodiment of her love for God and for the church. She had an awareness of the sacred nature of the forms of worship, and the connection of memory, meaning, shared experiences and relationships—and she felt the pain of the brokenness. I keep that chalice in my office as a reminder of the depth of meaning of worship for the people I am privileged to lead.

I know the importance of worship, and I am aware of the depth of feelings surrounding this important dimension of Christian life. I recognize the struggles of congregations as they seek to worship faithfully in this time of great change. I know that worship is the heart of the church's life, health, and effectiveness. Contained in our acts of worship are emotions, thoughts, meanings, and memories that are life itself. In some ways, *I see the image of the broken chalice superimposed upon our struggles surrounding worship. We are broken over issues of style and form, and at times we argue over which piece of the broken chalice is the most important.*

An emotional expression of this brokenness exists in churches engaged in the "Worship Wars." Under banners of "Contemporary" and "Traditional" church people choose up sides. Congregations and families are torn apart as the "war" rages. There is, however, a spirit of hope transcending these two extremes that longs for an end to these wars and a creative and faithful resolution of the tension. The cover of this resource shows raindrops hitting the water, becoming part of the larger body, creating ripples of change on the surface. Our diverse individual expressions of worship vary in size and shape. Like distinct raindrops, all of our worship finds its source and goal in the deep pool of God's presence and activity. *ReConnecting Worship* invites us to go deeper, reconnecting us to the purposes and the practices of worship. It invites us to reconnect with worship as an activity of the Body of Christ and to claim our place in the life of worship. As we reconnect with the heart of the church, our experience is enriched and the presence of God is made manifest in powerful ways.

This resource is designed as a group process to enable rich discussion around the issues of innovation, creativity, faithfulness and change. Participants read information, watch video segments of teaching, storytelling, and images of worship and change, and then reflect together on the ideas and implications that emerge. During each week, between group sessions, participants engage in a series of activities designed to integrate the weekly readings with daily life. Also included in the kit, you will find the book *ReKindling Your Music Ministry*. This book specifically addresses one of the most discussed ministry areas in the church in regards to worship—the music ministry. *ReConnecting Worship* does not specifically address the issue of the music ministry so *ReKindling Your Music Ministry* is included as a supplement to the *ReConnecting Worship* process. The approach discussed in the book can also be effective for those leading teams in various areas of worship ministries.

ReConnecting Worship is designed as a tool for churches to help people come to the table for discussion and learning about faithful innovation. It is possible to value the contributions and guidance of the cloud of witnesses that has gone before, respecting the contributions of generations of leaders who have worked to provide the church with patterns for faithful worship, while being open to the emerging innovations. The format will help diverse concerns emerge, so diverse styles of worship are respected, valued, and encouraged. The kit contains suggestions for effective approaches to planning and celebrating that can enhance worship in any congregation, regardless of stylistic approach. The process will be challenging as well as rewarding. It is not a "quick fix" or a "paint-by-numbers" approach. It seeks instead to deepen the knowledge and experience of the participants and to invite conversation about the meaning beneath the methods. At this critical time in the life of the church, we cannot afford to be passive. It is time to approach the planning of and participation in worship with the deep creativity, reverence, and a sense of the sacred that is required when handling holy moments.

You are holding this book for a reason.

You love worship.

You love God and the church.

You feel the tension, and you want to be both faithful and effective, and with God's help, are up to the challenge.

If we approach our connection to God with open minds, open hearts, and open spirits, God will bless us and lead us to a richer, deeper experience and expression of the act of worship. Whether you are studying worship as part of a leadership group or as a small group that wants to know more about our connection to God, we pray that this resource will nourish and increase your awareness of God's love.

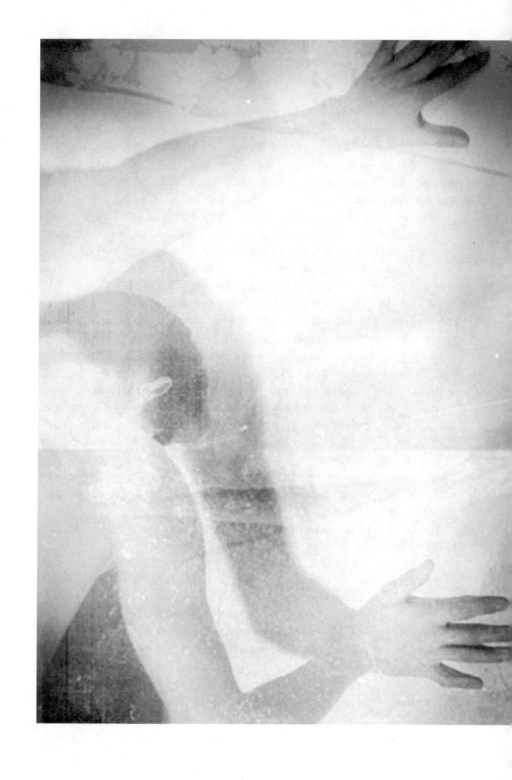

Chapter One
Embrace the Tension

I love worship.

I love the sound of water pouring as we prepare to welcome someone into the life of the church through the sacrament of Baptism. I love the sharing of the loaf and the cup in the sacrament of holy communion.

I love the sounds of children singing simple songs of faith. I love the sight of candles burning on the altar, and the sparkle in the eye of the young acolyte as the light moves both in and out of the worship area.

I love the creativity that has been expressed throughout the ages in the creation of great centers of worship, architectural marvels, every aspect of which tells the story of God. I love the sounds of music as they reverberate in sacred spaces, focusing my heart toward God. I love the simplicity of wooden chapels with the ringing sound of an old piano and the familiar words of soulful hymns.

I love the way that worship shapes me and shapes the community, inspiring us to guide others with God's light. I love the way the Word of God is proclaimed—the Bread of Life broken to remind me that I have a mission beyond myself, that I am chosen by God to love and serve so that I build up Christ's Body in the world and participate in the bringing of comfort, hope, reconciliation, and peace.

Engaging in the act of worship is what I love most. As I enter into that activity, I am choosing to step into a reality that is shared with Christians throughout the ages and with all those who gather to lift voices and turn eyes and hearts toward God. In worship, I am choosing to participate in an activity that reminds me and all who have gathered that there is meaning in the world, that there is hope, that there is something more than my worries and weaknesses, that God is real and that we will never be alone.

I love worship, and I believe that you share this love, which is why you have entered into the *ReConnecting Worship* process. While developing this study guide and video, I prayed for the church, I prayed for you, and I prayed for the generations who will be touched and transformed by the vital and creative worship of God, worship that will continue from generation to generation.

As you embark, I invite you to pause and share in this act of prayer. I encourage you to make this experience an offering of love to God for the sake of the hearts, minds, and souls of those in your congregation and of those who are being drawn toward God when they choose to visit with God in your house of worship.

As you pray the following words, allow your heart, mind, and spirit to be open to God:

Loving and creative God,

You knew me before I was created, and you brought me to this place. You created me with a desire that can find fulfillment only in an active relationship with you. You created me to worship you with all of my heart, mind, soul, and strength. Thank you for the gift of worship, especially the joy and fulfillment it brings to me and to my congregation.

Throughout the ages, you have called people to worship and to faithfulness. Times have brought great changes to our life and experience. We have become a people of many languages as your message and community have spread across time and cultures. Yet in the middle of this process of change, which results in the amazing diversity of your children, much has remained firm. Your love, your calling, your grace, and your presence remain constant and endure forever.

I come to you now, asking for clarity and renewal. I see the brokenness and division that is present in this world, and I know it brings you pain. Sometimes, I share in the brokenness and division that exists among your people. Forgive us. Forgive me.

I ask that you touch and shape my heart and mind so I become an instrument of your work in this world. Help me, God, during these next few weeks to open my heart and mind to you, so I might see clearly what you are saying to me. Touch me, O God, with your gentle and transforming power, so my heart might be an open vessel, ready to receive the gifts you are pouring out. Create in me a clean heart, and awaken a passion for those who long to worship you in Spirit and in truth, as well as those who may soon know you.

I pray in the name of Jesus Christ who came to us in our imperfection and brokenness to call us back to you and to create a new body, a reconnection with a shattered humanity that is unified in you.

Amen.

Perhaps you have been part of a conversation about change in worship. Change may be something energizes you, or it may be something that frightens you. Worship may be something you feel passionate about, positively or negatively, or it may be something that you would rather not think about. Whatever your experience with this conversation, it is not something that can be ignored if we value the health and wholeness of the church in the coming years.

I have spoken with thousands of pastors and unpaid church leaders about this issue. I have had conversations with professors, authors, worship leaders, musicians, pastors of churches of all different sizes and settings, new church developers, a variety of church leaders and congregation members (new and established, old and young), as well as many people who are looking in from outside the church. Two common themes surface in these conversations: 1) People feel strongly about worship, and 2) Great tension surrounds the notion of change.

As we become conversant with some of the issues facing the church in this time of great social and cultural change, listening is a vital skill to cultivate. Deep listening mitigates conflict, but more importantly it is evidence of the humility that God anticipates in worship. As we look beyond our immediate situation and hear from others in similar and different situations, we will develop an awareness of some of the real issues in our struggle. And perhaps, with the guidance of the Holy Spirit, we will be allowed to open ourselves truly to hearing the heartfelt struggles that come from faithful, passionate, and committed Christians. These are people who, like each of us, love to worship God, and who also feel the mounting tension between culture and tradition.

Before I introduce you to these congregations, let's address two terms that seem to be "hot buttons" in the conversation. These two widely used terms have been the source of a great deal of tension in the discussion of worship over the past twenty years. The words *traditional* and *contemporary* are used as if we share a definition in common. The truth is that these terms have become heavily value-laden and are always used from a particular interpretation to preserve one meaning or another.

For instance, those who oppose new forms of worship often use the term *traditional* in a positive light to mean "the way we do it," and the term *contemporary* in a negative light to mean "the way others do it." The reverse is also true. Those who favor a style other than the predominant worship format in their congregation might refer to *traditional* in a negative light meaning "the old way" and the term *contemporary* in a positive light to mean "the way we do it," or the new way. *Contemporary* and *traditional* are actually much more complex terms. Many forms of worship, old and new, contain elements of tradition as well as contemporary features found in the emerging culture.

In a later chapter we will explore some of the deeper meanings of these terms and the worship patterns and sources they represent, but for the sake of clarity, let's define these terms:

Traditional—Worship with printed prayers and responses, congregational singing primarily from a denominational hymnal, and "special music," either solo or choral, accompanied mostly by piano or organ.

Contemporary—Worship with little printed liturgy (though the song lyrics are often projected), using congregational singing and "special music" that draws from resources outside denominational hymnals, accompanied by a variety of instruments, usually piano, guitar, bass, and drums.

Obviously there is room for much variety and diversity in the worship styles represented by either of these broad definitions. The "traditional" service might be "high church" and very formal with anthems from eighteenth-century composers, or it might be based in the *Cokesbury Hymnal*, or *Hymns from the Family of God*, with choral anthems from the nineteenth or twentieth centuries. The contemporary service might be an edgy rock-and-roll service with poetry readings, video, and drama, or it could be a more folk-music style with a campmeeting feel.

With such a wide range of practice found in each of these terms, let us visit several churches involved in the discussion of worship and the tension between tradition and innovation. As we listen in on their conversations, notice which voices are familiar. Also, watch for opportunities or instances of either cooperation or conflict.

Church One

Identity: Established downtown church with a long history of excellent traditional, liturgical worship.

Situation: This church, a "flagship church" of the denomination, has moved through times of growth and decline and stabilized over the past few years after a new pastor arrived. New educational initiatives are in place to meet the needs of the new members. They are building buildings to house the growth in ministry activity and to make room for those who are yet to come. The choir director is a well-known and accomplished leader who has a preference for classical music.

Motivated by internal voices of some of the younger members as well as a desire to "speak a language" more accessible to those outside the church, the church started an alternative "contemporary" service. The new service is located outside the main sanctuary in an informal venue and makes use of a more popular form of music. The new service has grown to more than 100 people in average worship attendance, many of whom have come from the existing congregation. Others come from outside the church or have returned after a period of inactivity.

Conversation: The pastor hears the voices of those in the congregation who desire a more contemporary service to reach the youth and younger adults, according to what they claim to prefer. He believes that a different form of worship might be more inviting to those who are yet to be reached, even though he is personally most comfortable in the traditional service. The choir director is openly dismissive of the new service as being "worship lite." Members of the church feel polarized by the conflict between the attitude of the choir director and the voices of those who prefer the new service.

Church Two

Identity: Old established historic church in a county seat town with a stable membership in a growing community.

Situation: The congregation had two worship services for many years. Both services were traditional in presentation, oriented to a prayerbook rhythm, and lectionary-driven in liturgical style. While the surrounding area grew in population, the church remained relatively static. Enough new members joined the church to replace those who relocated or died. Even though the church is located less than a mile away from a university, very few young adults participate in the life of the congregation. Some of the members of the congregation express interest in starting an alternative service to reach younger generations using contemporary music, video, and projection technology.

The pastor researched different settings where alternative worship styles were implemented and organized a team to design and implement the new service by using the best elements of what he had learned and experienced. Members of the existing services were assured that the new service would not replace their current style of worship. The new service would be tried as an experiment to see if a new worship form proved viable and had the desired result of reaching the younger generations currently not attending.

The team organized musicians and others to assist in the planning and implementation of the new service, taking into account ushers, technicians to run the video projection and sound equipment, and hospitality ministries. A series of mailings was used to promote the new service to the surrounding community. The team worked with the pastor to design the worship experiences. The pastor continued to develop all of the worship services using the pattern of the lectionary.

Within one year, the new service was the same size as the larger of the two more traditional services, with more than 70 percent of its participants previously not connected to the church. The rapid growth created new problems for a church accustomed to stasis. There was not enough parking. The youth and children's programs, as well as the adult Sunday school program, had to be expanded to meet the needs of the large number of new members.

Conversation: At first, voices were heard from the participants in the traditional service, reacting to the inconvenience caused by the large number of new people. Others expressed concern that some of the members of the existing services were moving over to the new service. Some of those who had made the move responded that there was more energy, excitement, and creativity in the new service, and that people were given an opportunity to participate in worship by using their gifts in ways that had not been available in the other services.

Those in the traditional services felt threatened by what they heard and expressed concern to the pastor and the church leadership. After a series of discussions, however, participants in the traditional services decided that complaining about the success of the new service was not productive and instead decided to work on the energy and creativity in their services. As more people became involved in working to increase the quality and energy of the traditional services, those too began to grow.

There is still tension over the lack of parking and the crowded educational space, but these are tensions that most churches would welcome.

Church Three

Identity: New congregation started in a growing suburban ring around a major southern city.

Situation: The community surrounding the new church was extremely varied in age, religious background, and cultural identity.

Many of the residents of the community had relocated to the area for employment. Because of the great variety of backgrounds represented, the pastor decided to start three different types of services to reach different groups of people.

She designed each service around the same theme, so the congregation, even though worshiping at different times, would experience the same Scripture and content. The differences were primarily stylistic, designed to attract people with different preferences. The earliest service was quiet and contemplative. The music was from a variety of styles, performed with simple acoustic instrumentation. Communion was a part of the service each week. The second service was a high-energy, spirited traditional service with robes, organ, and hymnals. The eleven o'clock service was more informal, using a variety of contemporary music styles accompanied by a combination of piano, drums, keyboards, guitars, and various wind and brass instruments.

Conversation: The participants in the different services seemed happy to have the choice of different styles. People gravitated to the service that brought them most clearly into God's presence. Some of the members attended one of the services almost exclusively, while others moved freely among all three. Some of the members reported that the variety of styles gave them the opportunity to choose according to their particular life situation. One woman shared that there were times when she felt very comfortable in the highly liturgical and formal service, but when she was going through a time of crisis and internal questioning she felt out of place and was happy to have the contemplative service, where she felt more peaceful and introspective and, thus, more able to engage God in worship.

The participants in all of the services were encouraged to interact in educational and congregational fellowship events so that they developed a common identity, rather than becoming three separate congregations with the same pastor meeting in the same building.

Church Four

Identity: A thriving forty-year-old church with an upper-middle-aged, middle-to-upper-class congregation in a large university town.

Situation: Church Four has one "high church" service, one service with a contemporary format, and one off-site service that meets in the bar of a restaurant the church obtained as an outreach center. The contemporary service and the off-site service are relatively new. The contemporary service replaced a traditional service that had been dwindling in attendance and now is equal to or larger than the later traditional service. The worship service that meets off-site is highly informal with a variety of musical styles ranging from Taizé to alternative rock, with various instrumentation including piano, percussion, guitars, and wind instruments. True to its intent, the off-site service is composed mainly of people who have no previous background in the church. However, it is noteworthy that some of the participants in this service have taken on leadership roles in the larger congregation.

Conversation: Some of the longer-term members of the congregation resent the new worship styles and see the off-site service as a faddish experiment that will pass. Some members still negatively react to the drums and projection equipment, which they insist be removed from the sanctuary before the traditional service begins. The participants in the contemporary service, some of whom have come from within the congregation and some of whom are new to the church, are happy with the new format yet feel uncomfortable with the resentment from the participants in the traditional service.

Participants from all age groups attend each of the services. One of the older members said to me, "That new worship isn't something that I enjoy, but it has gotten my grandchildren to participate in church. I don't have to like the style, but I support it because it works."

Church Five

Identity: A new church designed from the ground up to reach younger generations who are staying away from existing churches.

Situation: Birthed as an outreach from a ten-year-old congregation, this church positions itself to reach the twenty-something generation that is not being drawn to the parent church. A young pastor (a member of the demographic being targeted) was engaged to lead in the formation of this congregation. He assembled a team of musicians and other creative individuals to design worship that is classic in structure, but makes use of modern music and forms of communication familiar to the people he is trying to reach. Video, drama, and lighting enhance the celebration of worship. The messages are scriptural and thematic, designed to address the questions and struggles of the congregation and those outside the church in similar situations.

While progressive in worship style, the pastor remains committed to his denominational heritage. In two years, this church has grown to more than 150 in average worship attendance.

Conversation: Much excitement and a high level of ownership persists among participants in this new congregation. While grateful to the parent church for the resources and encouragement provided, members have committed themselves to birthing another church within five years. Even though the worship styles of the two congregations are vastly different, relationships are good between them and a mutual sense of excitement emerges from their close relationship.

Church Six

Identity: A large church, with a little more than a decade of history, that strives to maintain connections among the various age and cultural groups, which make up the congregation and the surrounding community.

Situation: Located on a piece of land between areas of poverty and affluence, this church seeks to provide a context for worship that welcomes, develops, and encourages people from extremely diverse life situations. The three worship experiences offered are identical and incorporate a variety of different styles and communication methods that together form a convergence of traditions. A creative worship team composed of people with backgrounds in various art forms including theater, visual arts, photography, classical and contemporary music, altar design, dance, and children's ministry work together to develop the worship services. Programs are in place to train children in various forms of artistic and technological expression, so they will have the tools to participate in worship design and leadership as they grow.

The gifts and talents of many members of the congregation are used in a variety of ways to contribute to the worship experience. The sacraments are valued highly in the congregation, and elements of history and tradition are lifted up as guiding principles for worship and congregational life. The congregation is made up of members from very different backgrounds. There is socioeconomic, political, generational, and educational diversity, as well as a tremendous diversity of previous church affiliation or lack thereof. The congregation has grown rapidly and has become one of the largest mainline churches in the area.

Conversation: Internal conversations include a high degree of positive reaction to the worship experiences because worship services express congregational identity, tradition, and innovation. Some participants who visit from other churches find the experience refreshing and engaging, while others long for something more familiar.

External conversations from surrounding churches of the same denominational background range from wanting to learn more about this convergence of worship patterns to reacting negatively and characterizing it as disloyal to tradition.

Church Seven

Identity: A small rural family church with traditional rural worship that draws from historic denominational resources.

Situation: This congregation, founded in the late 1800s, is composed mainly of longtime residents of the small community. It is a close-knit congregation with an informal, traditional style. Music is mostly from denominational resources, and the instrumentation for worship is an acoustic piano. Occasionally one of the members shares a special piece of music accompanied by a guitar. The music of choice for the small choir tends toward country gospel. This community loves its worship style. The church, however, is aging, with few young people staying in the community.

Conversation: The conversation within this church does not involve worship style because the community is relatively homogenous and established. Many, however, wonder how long the church will remain open because of its aging membership, increasing number of funerals, and lack of new members.

Church Eight

Identity: A declining church in a small town surrounded with urban sprawl from a nearby metropolitan area.

Situation: The congregation feels threatened by numerical decline after a period of strong growth. Members are longing for the previous days of vitality and growth, yet are turning inward and focusing on negatives, rather than what it might take to reverse their decline. Across the street is a large church of another denomination that is exploding with growth. The neighboring church has changed worship styles completely and is drawing many of the new people who are moving into town.

Conversation: People in this congregation are in survival mode and are defensive about their worship style. They resent the "success" of the church across the street that is "taking all of the young people." They are openly hostile toward the idea of alternative forms of worship. New worship styles seem to be the scapegoat for their problems. They are adamant about maintaining things as they are, even though they find little joy in worship. Their focus is on the glory days of several years ago. People are conflicted and inwardly focused. The goals posted on the walls around the church begin with, "Pay off debt." The new pastor is trying to build small successes in the congregation, hoping church members might gain a foothold in order to climb out of the malaise.

Church Nine

Identity: A county seat church built in the 1900s by wealthy families in the region. Proud of its great domed marble sanctuary, the church has been a place of prestige for pastors and for members.

Situation: As transportation routes shifted, bypassing the county seat with a new interstate, the town gradually began to decline. The church was able to sustain a high salary for its pastor and a quality high-church music program, but attendance in the congregation followed the pattern of the population. As the decline became more pronounced, this congregation, like Church Eight, began to turn inward and enter into survival mode. The problems of the church were blamed on the new interstate. The internal attitude of the congregation shifted into blaming and anger.

It appeared that the congregation was headed down the path of so many other congregations, in a spiral of decline, until a group of committed and innovative lay members decided to try something different. These lay people believed that even though the town was in decline, there were still plenty of people who didn't attend church at all. In fact, the church had a constant stream of visitors to worship, although few of the visitors returned for a second visit, and those who did rarely joined. After making several contacts with many of the visitors, the group began to see a pattern. The most common response when asked why they did not return was, "We didn't feel at home in the worship service. It was depressing."

The group of lay people began to dream of a new worship service. They wanted to develop a service that had a greater degree of hopefulness, flow, and energy. They envisioned a service with many elements from their tradition and the addition of a different style of music, more congregational participation, and a focus on prayer. At first the pastor was resistant to the dream of the lay group. He saw contemporary forms of worship as "beneath a church of this station." As one who stood for faithfulness to tradition, he was worried about his reputation. As their excitement increased, however, he decided that blocking the group and standing in the way of the new service was not a battle he wanted to fight. While not actively supportive of the service, he agreed to preach for it.

The group took to the new endeavor with great energy and creativity. They recruited musical leadership, formed a creative ministry team, and developed a strategy for the new service. The service was launched and experienced moderate success, until the pastor moved on the career ladder and another pastor who was supportive of the new service came to serve the church. The service now fills the traditional old sanctuary to capacity. Financial giving is up, with 60 percent of the church's growing budget coming from participants in the new service. Sunday school rooms and nurseries that had long been unused are now full. Energy and life have returned to a congregation that appeared to be on its way to serious and perhaps terminal decline.

Conversation: Many of the older members have been vocally opposed to the creation of the new service. At first they claimed that it was not necessary and would be a waste of the church's time and resources. When it started and began to grow, their complaints changed. They argued that the people who were coming were there only to be entertained and to take, not give. When the new members of the church demonstrated their commitment by increased giving, the resisters countered that the new folks come to worship but they don't come to Sunday school, and "we are still having to do all of the work." Then, Sunday school attendance increased, mission programs began to thrive, the church opened a feeding ministry to serve those in the community who were struggling financially, and new members began to take on positions of leadership on church boards and committees. The opponents moaned that others were "taking over."

Gradually the voices of the opponents became softer and softer, and many who had been skeptical had a change of heart. They still preferred their more traditional service, but they began to see the new service not as competition but rather another successful ministry in the church. There are still some vocal opponents, but for the most part the church is learning to work together even though they worship in different ways.

Church Ten: *Your* church

Take a moment to reflect on your church. How would you describe your congregation's *identity, situation,* and *worship style?*

Identity:

_____

_____

_____

What are the characteristics of your congregation's particular situation as it concerns worship and change?

Situation:

_____

_____

_____

What are the voices that emerge in your mind when you consider people in your church and those you are called to reach?

Conversation:

_____

_____

_____

Wailing and Cheering

In the video, we remembered the tension in the Israelite community during the rebuilding of the Second Temple. This tension is similar to the tension between those in our churches who contend that we need not provide new forms of worship and ministry and those in our churches who excitedly pursue the creation of newer models. These temple-building-people-of-God had a choice to make. They could choose to remain in conflict based on memory and emotion, or they could find out how to love one another and work together as old and new converged. This convergence was enriched and shaped by the past and born from current realities and the need for faithful innovation. They decided to move past the *howling* and work together to continue the restoration of the Temple. In essence, there was at once a *reconnection* with their history and purpose and a reconnection with the reality of their shared situation. Did the nature of the worship of the people of God change? Yes, it did. It has been changing ever since. The core focus of worship does not change—God is always at the center—but the forms change, whether we like it or not. They change. This same situation and choice is the foundation for our experience in *ReConnecting Worship*.

We are in the midst of a time of drastic change, which is correlated with an alarming decline in church attendance. Added to this crisis is internal tension between those who, at the extremes, would hold fast to tradition at the expense of effectiveness, and those who are ready to dispose of tradition for the sake of relevance, at the expense of continuity and theological integrity. As we face this challenging period in our life as a church, we can learn from the words of the encouraging hymn, "Once to Every Man and Nation."

New occasions teach new duties,
Time makes ancient good uncouth;
They must upward still and onward,
Who would keep abreast of truth.[1]

As the church seeks to discern how best to shape itself in the emerging century, the question is not helpfully presented as a choice between traditional and contemporary forms of expression. It is much more mature to describe *a choice between a dynamic and productive use of tension or a destructive reaction to that same tension.* The solution to this difficult struggle is not found in any one particular form but in a recovery of the original identity of the church as the people of God.

Imagine a scene in which there is an encounter between two ordained ministers who are arguing about liturgical innovation and tradition, representing the dynamic of today's *"worship wars."* I hear them in heated discussion—each passionate about his or her own perspective. Into that tense situation appears Jesus. "Let's ask him," they both say at once (each believing, of course, in the depths of his being that he is right and that Jesus' answer would prove the other's folly).

Minister One: "Jesus, shouldn't we keep the tradition and the liturgy of the church pure, and shouldn't the music we use be time-honored and reflect the beauty and complexity of your creative and redeeming work?"

Minister Two: "Jesus, shouldn't we, like Paul, do anything that needs to be done to reach out to those who don't understand our traditions and culture, and help them to know you and worship you in their own native tongue and cultural context?"

In this scene, Jesus might pause for a long moment as if considering his answer to this complex line of questioning. After a few moments, he would speak, saying, "Do you love me?"

"Of course I love you," the two clergy would reply.

"Then feed my sheep."

I imagine Jesus not trying to avoid the conversation but reframe it. The issue is not choosing sides and fighting to see which style wins, but instead determining the most effective way to "feed the sheep" who are cheering, wailing, or swimming in the salt water of contemporary culture.

White Water

I remember the tension of white-water canoeing. There was always a great period of anticipation and preparation. We had to decide where we were going. We needed to know river levels and weather patterns. We packed equipment and canoes. We almost always departed before dawn to make the trip to the river's entrance. Equipment ready . . . life-jackets on . . . knee pads fastened . . . helmets handy . . . paddles in hand . . . pushing off into the gentle current.

For a time, the canoe glided smoothly across the surface of the water, surrounded by canyon walls of colored foliage and beautiful nature. Occasionally the current would pick up, and the sense of anticipation would grow as the heartbeat quickened. There was a stirring and excitement, minds quickened, laughter erupted, and a sense of common mission and adventure was pervasive. We were prepared and moving toward the goal—the white water.

As the canoes approached the difficult sections, the degree of focus and seriousness increased. Straps were tightened . . . helmets checked . . . and hands grasped paddles more tightly. Sometimes, if the rapids were particularly large, we would pull to the side to survey them and chart a course, prior to plunging in. Sometimes, they would appear almost unexpectedly—around a bend—and we were forced to react and respond as best we could, paddling through the raging water.

White-water travel is a provocative experience. When we are in it, it is exhilarating, but our focus constantly changes. When we are outside of the rapids, we relax and focus on the beautiful surroundings, remembering the previous challenges, and we dream of what is around the bend. When we are in the churning currents, we can focus only on what needs to be done right then—to get us through this wave and past that set of rocks, so we don't capsize and swamp the boat. *The goal is not to fight the river but to find the best way to move in concert with its energy.* Stroke-by-stroke, turn-by-turn, white knuckles grasping paddles, gritted teeth and pounding hearts, time becomes compressed into an intense series of adrenaline-filled immediate moments.

Then, as quickly as it began, it stops and the river widens again, the sound of the rushing water fades in the distance and flushed faces return to normal—but with broader smiles. With the immediate danger behind us and the shared accomplishment filling our hearts, the horizons broaden. We are free to laugh and joke and plan and remember once again—until the next white water—the reason we came to the river in the first place.

Sometimes I feel like our journey together—this unfolding adventure of worship—is much like a trip down the river. There is so much preparation and planning. There are times of great calm, laughter, memory, and dreaming, and there are times of negotiating the white water of change. Right now, as we enter this time of tension and emerging culture, it seems as if things are moving faster and that more effort is required to keep heading in the right direction.

As a pastor (one who is trained to be a river guide), I would encourage churches to understand that we are in a white water time, so we can be ready for this ride. If we are not ready, we can become frightened, uncomfortable, injured, or thrown from the sanctuary of the boat. If we are ready and aware that we are entering the rapids, times may get crazy, but it can be a great ride. We need all hands ready at the paddles. We need focus, strength, and prayer. We need to work as teams with coordination and communication. We need not fight against the river of change, but find the best way to move in concert with its energy.

Over the next few weeks, we will explore several of the currents and tensions around us in our continuing journey of worshiping together, examining how to balance the importance of tradition with the need for innovation. We may experience some turbulence, requiring the ability to react quickly and work together to keep moving forward, but I know we can do it. The people of God have been down similar rivers. It is part of the great adventure. So, get ready for the ride of your lives—and let the river flow.

Chapter One Connections

Each week, the "Connections" section will provide you with the opportunity to integrate the weekly reading with daily life. Included in the "Connections" section you will find a Planting suggestion designed for persons starting new churches, as well as 'e' ventures for those wanting to enhance the experience via the Internet.

Use a journal to record new ways in which you experience or encounter God through the week. Reflect upon those tensions you see within your own congregation. Where do you find yourself in the tension? Do you find yourself willing to move forward into a new future or do you find yourself afraid of the unknown? We have organized these activities into four categories: prayer, presence, gifts, and service. As you participate, turn up your awareness radar. Listen for what God might be speaking to you. Make notes to help you remember and better prepare you for discussing these experiences together.

Prayer

Pray for those you identified in the group activity at the beginning of session one. Pray for those weeping and those rejoicing in change. Pray for those in the varying age groups that surfaced in your discussion. Pray for those beyond the walls of your congregation who have not yet experienced God.

For each question in the group discussion activity, identify, by name, someone you know personally who fits each category. Let your prayer for this specific individual serve as a personal representative for each group as you pray throughout the week. In the space below write their initials or something that reminds you of them to guide your prayer time.

Planting

Consider the identity, situation, and worship style for which you would like to be known for as a congregation in five years. Consider how your new church start will incorporate aquarium dwellers, aquarium visitors, and saltwater swimmers.

Aquarium Dwellers   **Aquarium Visitors**   **Saltwater Swimmers**

Presence

As you begin this study, reflect on your worship experience as a child or youth. What elements were important to your experience? Was there a certain song or hymn that you especially loved? Was there a liturgical response with which you connected? Was it children's time, the sermon, or the memory of those in worship that takes you back to a positive memory? Think about how your memories have shaped your participation in and connection to worship today.

If you did not attend church or worship as a young person, what occupied that time for you and your family? While many of your friends may have been attending church, what activities were important to your family? In reflection, how did this time help to mold and shape you as an individual? When did it become important for you to connect to a community of faith?

Find some tangible representation and take it with you to your next *ReConnecting Worship* session. This may be as simple as writing the words down to a favorite prayer in your journal or pulling out an old Bible from a box of memories. You might bring a picnic basket if your memory of worship is associated with the fellowship of "dinner on the grounds" after the service; you might bring a lifepreserver if your memory of "Sunday" is spending the day with your family on the lake. You will have the opportunity to share this memory with the group next week.

Gifts

Think back to the discussion from the video on the aquarium dwellers, the aquarium visitors, and the saltwater swimmers. As you consider each group, what gifts and abilities might they contribute to the worshiping community? How do aquarium dwellers, those who have participated in the life of the faith community over many years, add depth to the community of faith? How do aquarium visitors, those who have some familiarity with congregational life, but have been shaped extensively by the outside culture, contribute? What might saltwater swimmers, those yet to participate in the gathered worshiping community, add to the worship experience?

Service

Identify someone in your own life who serves you during the week. It might be the person who delivers your mail. It might be the person who teaches your child at school or at church. It might be a friend or loved one. It might be the cashier at the corner store who hands you a receipt and change with a smile. Whoever it is, find a way to say thank you to that person this week. It might be with words, a card, or a special gift. In some way, acknowledge another individual to indicate that what he or she does makes a difference in your life.

'e' ventures

This week explore several church websites. What can you determine about each individual church's *identity, situation, and worship style* from the website? How is each church's theological perspective conveyed through the websites? Use a search engine (such as www.google.com) to locate a list of churches in your particular city or state. Also, see what church websites you might locate that are distanced from your particular location. Several sites are listed here if you need a place to begin:
(www.thegardenchurch.org, www.kingdombuilder.com, www.kum-cgw.org, www.marshillchurch.org, www.saddleback.com,
www.gingamsburg.org,
www.joyonline.org).

Session One Video

The video segment on the DVD or VHS in the *ReConnecting Worship Kit* that corresponds to this chapter is Session One: *Finding Common Ground and Renaming the Problem*. You will have already viewed the video when you work on these "connections" at home.

Chapter Two
The Purpose
of Worship

A member of our church staff is the mother of a little boy who asks "Why?" about everything. "Why does the sun shine?" "Why does rice grow like it does?" "Why do I have to take a bath?" "Why do you have to go to work?" "Why are there bad people?" "Why do I have to drink all my milk?" When she finally became flabbergasted with his questions, she asked a question of her own: "Why do you have to keep asking so many questions?" She hoped that somehow this question might get him to stop asking, if only for a few moments. The boy, however, was one step ahead of her. He had the answer to her question: "Because God made me that way."

Can you sense her response?

It was probably frustrating for this young mother, but she couldn't refute his answer. He was right, and she knew it.

Later, she decided that she might try that same approach with him. When he asked, "Mom, why is there up and down?" here was her chance. "Well, son, because God made it that way." She felt satisfied and imagined that he might go about his business. Of course, that didn't happen. He came back with yet another question: "Mom, why did God make it that way?"

This child is destined to be a philosopher.

God did make us with inquisitive minds. We want to understand. We want to know, especially when we are young. Sometimes, as we grow older and settle into the routines of life, we forget why we do things the way we do. We begin to operate on autopilot. Sometimes we even forget why it is that we do things at all. Sometimes we do things because we have been taught that they are "the right thing to do," and often we fail to examine why.

In this section, we look together at the *why* of worship. We can separate this question into three parts: Why do we worship? For whom is worship? And what are the desired outcomes of the *ReConnecting Worship* process?

Why do we worship?

Why do we worship? Well, it should not be to get a boost for the coming week, although that sometimes happens. It should not be to make sure the church stays open, although if enough people stopped worshiping, the church would close. We don't worship to be seen at church, or at least I hope that isn't our motivation. The purpose should not be to promote a particular style, encourage "brand loyalty," or maintain a particular historical format.

The reason we gather for worship is:

To celebrate and honor God.
To engage and build up the congregation to live out Christian disci-
*   pleship.*
To provide hospitable communication that welcomes others into a
*   fresh experience of and relationship with the living God.*

Worshiping is like checking a compass to keep us oriented toward God and God's purposes for our lives. Navigators do not check a compass because it is entertaining, or because it is a really attractive compass, or because "it is the same kind of compass my great-great-grandfather had," or because "that's the way we've always done it." Navigators check the compass to orient themselves toward their intended destination. All worship should find its origin in this purpose. Every ritual and litany, every song or drama, every sermon or sacrament exists to orient God's people toward God and to build communal life around that shared orientation. Each act of worship connects us to God's "Why."

An example of a living "Why" ritual

I deeply appreciate the setting of the Passover meal in Judaism. It is a symbolic meal designed to help answer those "Why" questions. "Why is this night different from all other nights?" "Why do we use the cup?" "Why do we eat bitter herbs?" As the questions are asked and answered, the children learn the story of the struggles of the people of God and the power of God to redeem, save, and continue to provide life. As parents share the answers to the story, they are reminded why they engage in this practice. It helps deepen their commitment to the faith story. This ritual is so important for connecting us to the history of God's activity that it was the setting Jesus chose to tell the disciples of his approaching death. He connected his death to this story and expanded it. He chose a connection to the past to unfold how his life is fulfillment of the same story. He reinterpreted this story as he added meaning to the ritual of the bread and the cup. He connected the old story with the emerging story, and through that connection he connects us to a new living "Why" ritual—the sacrament of Holy Communion.

The "Why" of worship can be understood if we take a look at the origins of the word:

wor·ship[2]
Etymology: Middle English *worshipe* worthiness, respect, reverence paid to a divine being, from Old English *weorthscipe* worthiness, respect, from *weorth* worthy, worth + -*scipe* -ship

Worship is acknowledging that God alone is of ultimate worth as the source and goal of human life. We often use a particular Scripture when addressing stewardship issues and that Scripture also has to do with where we ascribe ultimate worth: "For where your treasure is, there your heart will be also." (Matthew 6:21) This Scripture definitely has application for our use of resources, but more than that it has to do with where we offer our worship. In the act of worship, we gather together to affirm that God is the ultimate presence, the source and goal of our lives. We worship because we know that, as the psalmist states: "The earth is the Lord's and all that is in it, the world, and those who live in it" (Psalm 24:1).

This truth is something that should not be taken for granted, but it is a memory that has grown dim in many settings. Worship often evolves into an act of ritual attendance; something that we do because it is a duty; something that is attended for social reasons; something that is done out of habit; something that makes us feel better; something that entertains us. The true *reason* we worship is to *reconnect* with the reality that this is God's world and our very life is a gift.

Worship is the antidote to our disease.

One of the things with which we struggle most in this culture and time is the disease of self-absorption, or self-centeredness. Tony Campolo calls the disease "Affluenza."[3] This orientation is something that shapes our perspectives on all that we do. In many cases we feel entitled to things rather than understanding that all things are a gift from God.

Worship sets us in a different story. It reminds us who we are, and to whom we belong. It reframes the context of our lives, so that we don't see ourselves in the story of economy and commerce, of needs and worries, traffic jams, and "what's for supper." Worship puts us in an all-encompassing story as part of the creation of a loving God who longs for us to live in relationship with that same living God.

The statement of faith from the United Church of Ganada illustrates this:

> We are not alone. We live in God's world.
> We believe in God:
>   who has created and is creating
>   who has come in Jesus, the Word made flesh,
>   to reconcile and make new,
>   who works in us and others by the Spirit.
> We trust in God.
> We are called to be the church:
>   to celebrate God's presence,
>   to love and serve others,
>   to seek justice and resist evil,
>   to proclaim Jesus crucified and risen,
>   our judge and our hope.
> In life in death, in life beyond death,
>   God is with us.
> We are not alone.
> Thanks be to God. Amen.

These words contain the core memory and perspective that we tap into through corporate worship.

In *Resident Aliens,* Stanley Hauerwas and William Willimon suggest that "All ministry can be evaluated by essentially liturgical criteria: How well does the act of ministry enable people to be with God? In worship, in preaching, in serving the Lord's Supper, in baptizing, the pastor receives the model whereby all other pastoral acts are to be judged, the pattern into which all other ministerial duties are to be fit, namely, orienting God's people to God."[4]

Who is worship for?

How many times have you heard, "I just don't feel like I'm being fed at this church. I have decided to look elsewhere." While our spiritual satisfaction is important, this should not be the leading concern. We attend worship not first for ourselves but for God.

Danish philosopher Søren Kierkegaard lived in a society in which the church was state sponsored. The church was supported by taxes and was an ingrained part of the society. While the existence of the church was guaranteed, the passion of the church was diminished because it didn't call for commitment or sacrifice on the part of members.

While attending a worship service, Kierkegaard reflected that worship had developed to resemble a theatrical performance. It appeared to him that the setting and activity of worship had taken on the form and attitude of the theatre. The congregation was an audience; the priest, musicians and other worshipers were the performers; and, at best, the role of God and the Holy Spirit was that of prompter. In this setting, the focus of worship was on the actions and words of those up front, and the purpose of worship seemed to be to engage and entertain the audience. In the words of the contemporary philosopher Whoopi Goldberg, who played the lead role in the movie *Sister Act*, the purpose was to "get some butts in the seats."

Kierkegaard offered a different perspective. He said that the audience for worship is not the congregation but God. God is the one to whom our worship is directed. It is not for entertainment. Participants are shaped, formed, and built up through worship, but those benefits are byproducts of an authentic worship of God. If God is the audience, then who are the actors? Kierkegaard says that the actors are the worshipers whose songs and prayers are offered for the audience of One.

The role of the priest, the preacher, the musicians, and other worship leaders becomes that of prompter. They exist to aid the gathered Body of Christ in performing the act of worship for the Holy One. Authentic worship reframes all of life, where we live, pray, work, and worship, as an offering to the audience of One, who alone is worthy of all praise and honor. Worship is to be directed to God.

Worship as drama directed to God is a provocative analogy, but an important dimension is lacking in this analogy. If a divine drama is performed for the audience of one, we miss the incarnational dimension that comes from the second person in the Trinity, Jesus Christ. Kierkegaard's image of worship provides for our offering of worship, commitment, and praise to God, and accounts for the activity of the Holy Spirit as the prompter for our actions (the one who leads us into all truth). However, if worship is to be a truly Christian activity, then we have to ask, "Where is Christ present?" Many would respond, "Christ is present in our worship with God as the risen one to whom we offer our praise."

While worship is to be focused on the Risen One, who is worthy of praise as we learn in the Book of Revelation, it is more important to remember that Christ is received in the act of worship as the Incarnate One.

Incarnation is a strange word for many of us. It is not something that we use on a regular basis. Incarnation is a theological word for God entering into human form; God becoming flesh in the person of Jesus Christ. This doctrine has many dimensions: 1) Christ became flesh and dwelt among us; 2) Christ died and rose again and expected the Church to live out his life of reconciliation and redemption in the world as the Body of Christ; and 3) Christ is present in the least, last, and lost, so our ministry to those beyond the church is actually ministry to Jesus himself.

Christ became flesh and dwelt among us.

God in Christ lived in flesh—"pitched tent" with us—not in a comfortable, detached Winnebago, but on the ground, in the dirt, and in the pain and joy and tears. God came to be with us. Isn't it amazing that the creator of the universe cared enough for creation to enter it with all of its imperfection, pain, hostility, and tears to show us the depth of God's love? (See John 1:14.) This is part of God's nature that is seen not only in the coming of Christ but also in the second creation story in Genesis 2:5-7. God, the creator of all, gathers up dust (dirt or clay) from the earth forms a human being, and breathes divine life into the new form. This is a God who has been and continues to be intimately involved in creation. This is a God who continues to pour divine life into us even though we are broken. This is the God of incarnation.

Christ died, rose again, and expects the Church to live out his life of reconciliation and redemption in the world as the Body of Christ.

As I participate in Christian community, I do not participate in a human organization or series of activities. Instead, I am knit together with other members of the Body of Christ, alive in the world. Worship becomes the activity of the continual resurrection and life of Christ in the world.

Christ is present in the least, last, and lost so that our ministry to those beyond the church is actually ministry to Jesus himself.

The image of the incarnation of Christ extends well beyond the walls of the Church. Matthew's church acknowledges how our worship will be evaluated at the end of time. "Then they also will answer, 'Lord, when was it that we saw you hungry or thirsty or a stranger or naked or sick or in prison, and did not take care of you?' Then he will answer them, 'Truly I tell you, just as you did not do it to one of the least of these, you did not do it to me.'" (Matthew 25:44-45)

Christ is present in the naked, the hungry, the imprisoned, and the thirsty. If our worship is to truly demonstrate our commitment to the Incarnate One, then our worship—in focus, hospitality, and direction—must be not only God-focused, but also focused on the presence of Christ in the least, last, and lost.

Worship isn't something that is simply done for God and inspired by the Holy Spirit; it is something that is done as the Body of Christ. Those gathered to worship are not merely performers in the activity of worship, engaging in a divine drama for an audience of One. Worshipers are the redeemed ones living out the reality of becoming the living Body of Christ in the world.

"Who is worship for?" We would answer: 1) Worship is for God; 2) Worship is for the worshiping community and for enabling the continual resurrection and life of the Body of Christ as the community of the baptized; 3) Worship is for others.

What are the desired outcomes of worship?

If we were designing a process for making a particular product, we would want to know what we were planning to make. If we were designing the curriculum for an elementary school, we would want to know at least the basic things we would hope all of the students graduating fifth grade would have learned. It is important to know the desired outcomes of any process. It is likewise important for us to know the desired outcomes of worship.

Worship develops intentional relationships with God.

Relationships require work. Anyone who has been married for any period of time knows that a marriage does not survive merely on the emotion that drew the two individuals together in the first place. Time moves on, and the demands of careers, children, community involve-ment, and extracurricular activities fill their lives and demand the attention of the married couple. Without careful attention, the rela-tionship can begin to diminish. I have heard on many occasions from people who were deeply in love but began to drift apart because of the activities and distractions of life: "I don't know how or when it hap-pened, but I feel like we are just two people who happen to share the same address and sleep in the same bed." For those who are commit-ted to strengthening the relationship and reconnecting with the love that drew them together in the first place, an effective practice is to develop a date night. That night is set aside for the couple to spend time with each other, free from other distractions, and to focus on building the relationship.

Of course it takes much more than a date night to sustain a relation-ship, but establishing a date night as a priority on the couple's calendar says, "This relationship is important enough for me to set aside time to ensure its health and survival." In many ways there is a similarity to this situation in the practice of worship. Committing to the practice of wor-ship implies that "This relationship with God and the Body of Christ is important enough for me to set aside time to ensure its health and sur-vival." Worship must be designed to help us focus on reconnecting with this relationship.

Worship educates and edifies.

Worship is the place where we hear again the stories of God and God's people. As we sing songs, hear sermons, and involve ourselves in liturgy and sacrament, we learn the stories and the doctrines of the faith. While worship is not primarily an intellectual venture, wor-shipers should grow in their knowledge of God and the ways in which this knowledge intersects and transforms life. The acts, songs, and words of worship play an important role in the education and forma-tion of the congregation.

Worshipers are to grow not only in knowledge, but also in the love of God and neighbor. Worshipers are not to be unchanged by their par-ticipation in worship. One test of the effectiveness of worship in build-ing disciples of Jesus Christ is to examine the lives of those who participate in worship. Are they growing as followers of Jesus Christ? Are the values of God's story becoming the guiding values of the lives of those in the congregation? Are they becoming more God-directed? Are they becoming more selfless and loving toward their neighbor?

I once served a church in which there were two men who seemed to hate each other. They had had an encounter many years before that left them resentful of each other and they were too stubborn to let go of their anger. They would sit in worship and scowl at each other. During the course of the years I served that congregation, I buried both of these men. I was saddened by the lack of forgiveness they showed toward one another and the joy they missed because they refused to participate in the forgiveness to which Christ called them. I spoke with each of them about their lack of forgiveness and invited them to move past this stumbling block in their Christian life, but they both refused. To this day, I hurt when I remember them coming to the communion table to share in the Lord's Supper, knowing that, while they were going through the motions of worship, they were not allowing the fundamental reality of the Grace of God to permeate their lives and their relationships.

We cannot force people to change, but we should lift up examples in the congregation of people who have received and offered grace and who have become transformed in the process. We know people who have come to the church broken, hurting, addicted, or in despair, and through their participation in worship have been truly changed. They came with hearts open and the desire to be remade by the power of Christ. They have shared in confession, heard and received words of pardon and assurance, listened to the holy words of Scripture, contemplated the words of sermons, and shared in the sacraments of baptism and communion. As they actively engaged worship as participation in the Kingdom of God, they were remade as disciples and filled with a life that was not their own but Christ's. As we shared those stories, others saw possibilities and began to believe a similar hope available to them. Worship became a place that embraced the expectation of transformation.

Worship heals and creates caring community.

A member of the congregation was facing major heart surgery. He had come to the church after a prolonged period of "wandering in the wilderness." In worship and Christian community, he had begun to experience new life in Christ and to grow as a disciple. He was using his gifts and abilities in woodworking to enhance worship and to serve others in the community by repairing houses and building wheelchair ramps for the homebound and handicapped. He had become a well-loved member of the community.

During the worship service on the day before his surgery, the children were gathered in the front of the worship area and ready for children's time. I asked this man to come and sit with us. He came forward and sat on the floor in the middle of the children. I told them the story of his coming to the church and what God was doing in his life. I then shared with them that he was going to have a very serious surgery the next day and that we needed to pray for his healing, asking God to strengthen and prepare him for the surgery and to guide the hands of the doctors and nurses who would be involved. I asked the children to place their hands on him, as was the practice in the early church, as we prayed for his healing. We prayed a simple prayer, the children repeating it line by line. When we finished praying, there was not a dry eye in the sanctuary.

As everyone returned to their seats, I reminded the congregation of the healing power of God, as well as our responsibility to "bear one another's burdens and thus fulfill the law of Christ." In that simple act, people were transformed. Our friend received a confidence that comes from the simple faith of children interceding on his behalf. He felt the healing, loving touch of children's hands as they lifted him in prayer. The children participated in an activity in worship that allowed them to share the real and tangible good news of the gospel and the hope for healing through the power of Christ. The congregation was reminded of the place of healing in the community of the faithful. As we shared in this activity in worship, the congregation was shaped as a caring community. Worship engages us in the activities that proclaim what we believe, and as we participate, we are formed.

Worship shares the story to invite a response.

While worship services are not to become venues for self-help lectures, they are experiences that express the call and expectations of gospel life. Worship services designed only to be socially correct or emotionally comforting miss the important nature of the call of Christ to repentance and commitment. The message of Christ is at times a message of comfort for those who are suffering, struggling, or lost. It is also a message that invites a turning. I have experienced worship services that were so completely focused on happiness with Jesus, without any recognition of the pain and struggles of the community, that I wondered whether I was in church or at a pep rally. I have also experienced worship services where the Scripture, liturgy, and music seemed to have no relationship to the sermon, and the sermon seemed more like a pastor's personal agenda than a proclamation of the gospel. If worship is truly to orient people toward God, then people will likely need to shift their orientation from something else. Worship services hold up the story of God's life and call for people to come in. The worshiping community must expect and be prepared for people to respond.

In the early 1700s, the great evangelist George Whitfield was leading revivals in the open air around Bristol, England. He was preaching the gospel to many listeners who were outside the church. There were many who were caught in the cycle of poverty and lack of education. There were many who worked oppressive schedules in the coal mines for little pay. Despair and alcoholism were widespread. The people needed to hear a message of hope and hear a call to a different and better life. Whitfield preached and called for response. The vast number of persons responding to the call overwhelmed him. His preaching was successful, but he had a problem. He had no support structure in place to nurture and educate, to care for and develop those who were reaching out and wanting to enter into the new life of which they had heard.

Whitfield contacted John Wesley, who joined the revival movement in Bristol. Together, they built support structures and networks of small discipleship formation groups to sustain the people as they journeyed into newness of life. Without these, the individual and social transformation that emerged from that revival might never have happened. This lesson provides important perspective and direction that can inform the purposeful outcomes of our worship.

Consider a worship service that was centered in the Scripture of how Elisha was called by Elijah. At the conclusion of the sermon, I asked, "In the ordinary times of your life, when you hear the calling of God to a new way of being, when you feel those internal stirrings of the Spirit beckoning you to come, how do you respond? You have the same choices before you as did Elisha. What would it mean for you to break the plow that ties you to your past? What would it mean if you gathered the community around you and said, 'From this day, I am changed?' Today, you hear the calling to a new life in Christ and this is your community. What are the plows you must leave behind?"

Following the sermon, the congregation shared Holy Communion, the meal that sealed the direction of Christ's life and called the disciples to follow in perpetual remembrance. At the end of the service, there was no dramatic altar call. There was no coercion or manipulation, but I invited anyone who had heard a call or experienced the movement of

God's Spirit in his or her life to meet with pastors and other church members. One man came and shared his struggle with an addiction to gambling. A woman came to share that she had just come from jail after being arrested for her second DWI. Another man came to inquire about the meaning of a dream in which he felt that God was prompting him in some way. We prayed with each person who came forward and helped them connect with other members of the community who would help them move toward God's hope for their lives. If the call to repentance and commitment had not been issued, and if the community had not expected a response, what would the outcome of the worship experience have been?

Sometimes the call is to forgive others as we have been forgiven. Sometimes the call is to participate more deeply in taking responsibility for our discipleship through education or spiritual development. Sometimes the call is to participate in real Christian community by opening one's home or participating in a small group for discipleship. Sometimes the call is to discover or deploy the gifts that God has given for service in or beyond the church. The call is not always for inward personal transformation. Sometimes the call is for a reorientation of the congregation's attention beyond themselves to the brokenness and need around them. Frequently in worship, the invitation or call is issued as an opportunity to serve beyond the walls of the church. It could be a call to provide funds, material, or effort to replace the roof on a disabled woman's house. The call could be to participate in the rebuilding of a house in a high-crime, high-poverty neighborhood in which interns can live while they work on their studies in community renewal. It could be to participate in the feeding ministry, tutoring ministry, or medical clinic that serves that same neighborhood a couple of miles from our church. The call is varied, but it should be included as a part of the gathering of the community for worship. We worship a God who calls us into relationship, calls us from bondage, calls us to enter a new story and a new life, and calls us to live beyond ourselves as bringers of the good news in word and deed.

In essence, then, the outcomes of worship are *to center and send* the congregation. Worship centers the congregation in the story and transforming power of God, who calls for and expects a response, and worship provides help and direction to those who respond. Worship also sends the congregation to live out the reality of their lives in God beyond the walls of the church. If these outcomes are desired, then we can build our worship experiences in order to enable those outcomes through whatever worship styles we use.

Perhaps we need a litany similar in format to that of the Passover Supper for remembering why it is that we worship. Perhaps we need a series of questions and answers that we can share in our homes around the table prior to coming to church, and prior to entering the world for work, school, or vocation. Instead of rushing to get dressed, yanking children from in front of the TV, or off of the video game, imagine what it would be like for families all across the world to gather together prior to worship as the Sabbath day begins and share in a litany like this:

A Christian liturgy that begins with Why?

Why do we worship?

We worship to honor God and to give thanks to God for giving us life.

Why do we share in the bread and cup?

We share the bread and the cup to connect us to the faith that was so important to Jesus, remembering the way God saved the Israelites and brought them out of slavery. We share the bread and the cup to remember Jesus' love for us, and his ultimate sacrifice, by which we are given new life.

Why do we focus on the cross?

We focus on the cross because it is, at once, a symbol of our human tendency towards self-centeredness and injustice, and a reminder of Jesus' death and resurrection, which offer us the possibility of abundant life in this world and in the world to come.

Why do we make our offerings?

We give our offerings to God to demonstrate that we know that God is our ultimate value in life, because we need to be free from our attachment to and dependence on money, to assist the poor, and to further the work of the Church, the Body of Christ in the world.

Perhaps we need an empty chair in the chancel so we can remember those who are not present with us—or a cardboard box to remember those who sleep in one, or an empty shopping cart to remember those who cannot afford food.

Why do we worship? Probably the best answer we can give echoes the words of the little boy I told you about at the beginning of this chapter: "We worship because God made us that way." We were created to love and worship God. Worship is the natural response to the presence, love, power, and activity of the God who created us, redeemed us, and sustains us in this life and the life to come.

Chapter Two Connections

Planting

With members of your core group, visit a worship service within your community. See if you can arrange an opportunity before or after the worship service to interview two to three members of the congregation. First, meet with a worship planner or leader (choir member, etc.) Second, visit with a long-term church member. Finally, speak with a youth, child, or church visitor. Ask them the questions under "Presence" in Chapter Two Connections. As you reflect upon the responses, consider how your new church will express the "why" of worship.

Prayer

Use the litany at the end of this chapter as a guided prayer before attending worship this week. You might do this with someone else or individually. Prayerfully reflect on the "why" of worship for you as an individual. Pray that God might connect you to a deeper sense of why you worship.

Presence

During the week, talk with three different people currently attending your worship service(s): someone in elementary school, someone in high school or college, and someone of an older generation. Ask them some of the following questions about worship and record their responses in your journal. When you return to the group next week, you will have the opportunity to share some of the responses.

1. Why do you attend worship?
2. What is most meaningful (or what is your favorite time) in the worship service?
3. At what point to you feel closest to God in worship?

Gifts

Reflect on your personal "worship history." On the timeline below or in your journal, chart your worship history. Use the example as a guide. Identify the congregations of which you have been part over the years. Identify the blocks of time you may have been in a particular role of leadership in worship. Next week you will use your timeline to share your worship history journey with the group.

Worship History Timeline Example:

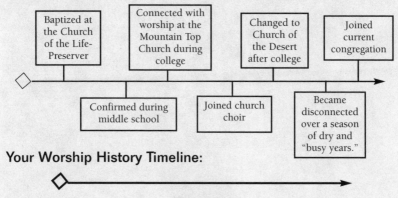

Your Worship History Timeline:

Service

Send a note or email to someone who has helped to shape your worship history. Let them know how their participation in worship has contributed to your own desire to participate in the creation and support of engaging worship for generations yet to come. Thank them for the effect they have had on your life.

'e' ventures

Visit www.gratefulness.org and click on "light a candle." Participate in this online activity of reflection and remembrance. Reflect on how you responded to this activity. Reflect on how this activity might be meaningful to someone who spends time online.

As you think about artifacts in your home and your church this week, imagine what digital artifacts might become part of the emerging generation's history.

Session Two Video

The video segment on the DVD or VHS in the *ReConnecting Worship Kit* that corresponds to this chapter is Session Two: *Mission, Tension, and the Great Commission.*

Chapter Three
Currents and
Tributaries

Understanding a person's family background can provide a great deal of insight into that person's perspective and behavior. I remember someone asking me about my mother and father. I told them my father was an ordained minister, a professor of social ethics and Wesley studies at a university, and a leader in the doctoral program. I explained that my mother was a kindergarten teacher and she loved to enter into the world of children, to help them learn, play, plant seeds, enjoy animals, paint, color, share stories, and develop their creative dimension for the enjoyment of life. The person responded, "So that's why you are the way you are." We can discover a lot about why we are the way we are and why we do what we do. We can gain a depth of understanding from reconnecting with our family identity.

I enjoy old family pictures. I like to look at pictures of relatives whom I know, from times before I was born. It is fascinating to look at pictures of relatives whom I never knew, but without whom I would not exist. Sometimes they are humorous, like the old movies my father has of his relatives at the lake in New Orleans, in their striped and oversized swimsuits, or pictures of my mother's relatives who came from Sweden and Austria and settled on a farm in Connecticut. As I gaze into the faces of those relatives, I try to imagine what their lives were like, what they were thinking about as the picture was taken, or what they dreamed of and worked for. Sometimes I am drawn to the characteristics of appearance and posture, and I marvel at the resemblance I see in my brother, my son, and myself. Family resemblance is passed one generation to another through the sharing of the same genes; changes come with the addition of new genes, and new family resemblances emerge. In some ways, the faces change, and in some ways there is a distinctive quality that remains the same. These people lived in different times and different places. Their interests and situations were different. What they drove and the way they worked were different. The people they loved and the mistakes they made were different. And yet, there is that resemblance. It is mixed in with other family lines, set in a different frame and a different location in time. Are they the same people? Of course they are not. Each birth is a life unto itself, with a separate identity, experience, and history. Yet even though they are unique and separate individuals, are they the same family? Yes, they are. This same dynamic is present in churches.

The movie *Pleasantville* is about two young people who are transported into a different world through the TV screen. They end up in the world of black-and-white TV in the 1950s. It is like the world of the Cleavers of *Leave it to Beaver* fame. Everything is pleasant. Everything is in its ideal place. People ask no questions. They seem content with living in a very small, well-defined, comfortable, changeless and passionless world. In this strange, isolated and limited place, when you approach the edge of the town, it begins again. There is no beyond. As the visitors from the "real world" begin to have an effect on Pleasantville, minds and lives begin to be opened, causing both excitement and difficulty. One of the visitors tells them that there are some places where "at the edge of town, the road just keeps going ..." The other students are shocked because they had never thought beyond their own town. The boundaries of their town were the boundaries of their world. They were used to one way of being and never even imagined something that might be different.

Sometimes we live so long in particular settings that we begin to assume that the whole world is like "here and now." This isn't usually intentional, and it doesn't imply shortsightedness or ignorance. Instead, horizons become limited by familiarity and routine.

The following section offers a fast-paced overview of the changing landscape of church culture. Imagine yourself in a hot air balloon, traveling through time with a wider perspective and observing the currents of change.

Two currents of historical development in North America are explored: 1) the process of church expansion and reactions to change in demographics and cultural development; and 2) the diverse perspectives and purposes that contributed to our various expressions of worship.

The process of church expansion

Christianity came to North America in different forms and for different reasons. One group of Christians came to the New World to escape religious persecution and to develop worship life and other expressions of church life free from the influence of oppressive government control. Another wave of Christian influence came in the form of missionary movements whose stated purpose was to evangelize the native people of the land, but who instead developed ministries of outreach to the immigrant inhabitants who were constantly moving westward to establish new frontiers and settle greater portions of the continent. As the frontier expanded westward, Methodist circuit riders and other traveling preachers, such as Baptists, would visit the new settlements and establish Christian communities. These communities frequently became small churches, made up of multiple generations of a few families. These churches became highly independent and lay-driven because clergy were always on the move, as they reached out to new areas and infrequently visited the congregations they had helped organize.

As the frontier became more settled and open to new waves of immigrants, churches were scattered throughout rural areas because society was still primarily agricultural. The rural areas were where people could be found. As more and more people moved into settled regions, towns began to spring up, and gradually churches developed in the new centers of population. Train travel and industrialization brought a new era of church development. With the rail system providing arteries for the rapid transportation of people and goods, trade began to flourish, and larger towns began to grow around significant rail stops. You can still see the evidence of this stage of our social development if you live in or visit some of these old "whistle-stop" towns.

My wife's grandmother was from one of these towns in Mississippi. It was a farm-to-market center and gradually grew into a thriving community. A great deal of wealth was generated in the area, especially by landowners who prospered because the rail system provided access to markets for the sale of their commodities. These landowners and the people who developed the support systems of the town joined churches. Because of their prosperity, they were able to build large and impressive church facilities. These "whistle-stop" churches thrived in the early part of the twentieth century. These towns and the farming communities were the primary centers of population growth, and churches grew there to serve the people. The town in which she lived has several large, impressive, mainline churches in prominent locations. The churches, however, no longer have congregations of the size to need or maintain the buildings. Changes occurred in the nation as a whole that caused these churches to experience serious declines.

Three things happened about the time of World War II that changed the dynamics of the distribution of population and the patterns of transportation. These had dramatic consequences for existing churches and new church development: construction of the interstate highway system, emergence of the automobile as the main mode of transportation for families, and the return of a generation of soldiers from the war with a subsequent boom in population.

The interstate system provided rapid access to many parts of the country that had previously been remote. It also provided an alternative method of transportation of goods from farm to market, leaving the agricultural industry much less dependent upon the rail system. With the reduced dependence on the rail systems, the whistle stop towns began to decline. Automobiles opened the door to a new pattern in population distribution. People no longer needed to cluster in big cities or whistle stop towns based on proximity to goods and services. People could simply get in the car and drive. A new cultural phenomenon exploded along with the growth of the post-war generation—the suburbs. New suburban developments sprang up all over the country, seemingly overnight. The church, as it had done in the days of frontier expansion, responded to this new population distribution by starting wave upon wave of new churches.

By the mid-1950s, the face of the church had changed dramatically, along with the dramatic changes that were happening throughout the nation. Suburban churches, with their new buildings, were filled by energetic young families with children in starched shirts, white dresses, and well-shined shoes. Mainline denominations flourished and built huge programs to support the tremendous growth in the churches, providing new hymnals, Sunday school literature, and training materials. While this new growth was taking place in the primarily white suburban churches and in city centers, rural churches and whistle-stop churches experienced decline. African-American churches experienced some growth during this time as well; however, the phenomenon of suburbanization and economic prosperity, for the most part, passed by the African-American community.

In the 1960s, changes occurred that had lasting effects on church growth and development. While suburban life was becoming increasingly prosperous, those who missed the wave of prosperity became increasingly impoverished. Crime began to increase, especially in the city centers. The increase in crime as well as the relocation of commercial centers closer to the suburbs and interstates led to a widespread fleeing of the city centers. During this time, too, an idealistic generation emerged to question the validity of institutions and accepted social norms. This generation rebelled against structure, organization, authority, and institution. The church was far from exempt from this rebellion. Droves of once starch-shirted, white-dressed children departed from church life to seek meaning and spirituality in a new youth movement. New forms of music developed rapidly, fed by an increased access to mass communication. While the general population continued to increase, mainline churches began to decline in attendance, as many members of an entire generation sought meaning and spirituality elsewhere. As Donald Miller states in *Reinventing American Protestantism*,

> Church attendance peaked in the 1950s, when 49 percent of the U.S. population indicated that they had attended religious service in the last seven days. Beginning in the early 1960s, attendance slowly declined until it bottomed out at 40 percent in the 1970s, and it has remained at approximately this level until the present.[5]

Although they stayed away from the institutional church, not all of the members of this post-war Baby Boom generation remained separated from Christianity. Combined with a hunger for spiritual connection, an informality characteristic of the generation, and a new form of guitar-driven music, a new Christian movement began in California. Members of the youth movement who converted to Christianity began to develop into what became known as the "Jesus people." These young Christians began to draw a following and organized evangelical churches that worshiped in an informal style with music from the folk and rock genres. Out of this movement that spread rapidly across the nation sprang new nondenominational churches.

Nondenominational churches emerged with a renewed fervor for evangelism and the quest for authentic spiritual experience. They rediscovered the small group movement that had been characteristic of the early church and also was the sustaining structure of the Wesleyan revival of the 1700s. This new wave of churches experimented with a combination of early Christianity and contemporary forms of expression designed to reach the large numbers of people who were avoiding mainline churches. In the 1980s, several new model churches were growing rapidly because of this

new methodology and were successfully gathering large numbers of con-
verts and incorporating them into a form of Christian community. As
churches such as Calvary Chapel in Costa Mesa, California, Saddleback
Community in Mission Viejo, California, and Willow Creek in South
Barrington, Illinois, grew into huge congregations and drew members and
participants from a large geographic region, other churches started to follow in their footsteps and organize churches for growth. Electronic projection, rock music, dramas, video presentations, and practical teaching
were incorporated into the worship services of these "new paradigm
churches." Soon, "church growth" was the buzz in many Christian circles
and many mainline churches jumped on the bandwagon.

However, other mainline churches remained largely unaware of the
transitions taking place in churches across the country. There was resistance to the church growth movement from some leaders in the mainline
for a variety of reasons. Some argued that the new churches had sold out
the gospel message for the sake of entertainment. Others claimed that
these new churches could draw a crowd, but they were not producing
disciples for Jesus Christ. Others argued that the focus of these churches
was too centered on the individual and lacked sensitivity to the social
dimensions of the gospel. In some cases, throughout the church growth
movement, some of these accusations were probably true. However, in
many situations new congregational forms were producing changed
lives, missional outreach, concern for the poor, and rapid growth
beyond anything the church had experienced in a long time.

The 1980s was the decade of the church growth movement, and it
showed great results in terms of building large congregations. As the
1980s gave way to the 1990s, a new area of concern arose. With many
congregations growing rapidly, large numbers of previously non-
Christian people and members from other churches and denominations
were assembled into communities that began to need new tools for discipleship and community building. They needed structure and resources
for education and leadership development. Almost by necessity the
focus changed from church growth to church health. Churches realized
that they could not sustain growth without developing the connecting
ligaments and systems to provide support. Organizations sprang up to
produce resources for discipleship development, spiritual gift discovery,
and small group training and implementation. While these churches
remained committed to evangelism, they began to focus on the health of
the congregation and the development of the lives of the members.

The turn of the century has seen a movement toward balance between evangelism and the spiritual health and vitality of the congregation. There is a renewed interest in ancient spiritual practices and a recovery of the reformation idea of the priesthood of all believers. A renewal of interest in the practice of the sacraments is also growing.

For many churches, changes happened so quickly and dramatically that they hardly knew what had happened. Others that tried to sort out all of the new information were left with their heads spinning. Some turned inward in an attempt to remain safe from the storms of change happening all around. Some churches were able to ride some of the waves of change and incorporate various elements of the emerging church culture. All in all, however, this rapid change has caused a great deal of uneasiness and agitation. It feels as if we have been in a blender on high speed, and then the blender was cut off. Now, we are trying to get our bearings again.

- Do you recognize any of these changes affecting your church or community?

  _____

  _____

Exhale for a moment, but don't completely relax. We have one more leg on this journey we still need to travel.

The currents of worship style

Like the old pictures that call me to reflection and imagination, certain "artifacts" stir my imagination as well. When I go home to my parents' house, I encounter several of these. There is the old Swedish Bible that has been part of the family for a long time. Higher on the bookshelf there is a strange-looking box. The top and bottom are wooden, and the sides, connected at the corners by vertical wooden supports, are metal, punched with holes. It looks like it might be a crude cage for some sort of animal. My father told me it was a bed warmer. It was designed to hold bricks that had been heated in the fireplace and then placed under the covers in the bed when the only sources of heat were the fireplace in the main room and the cast iron, wood-burning stove in the kitchen. There is a huge, hand-carved mortar and pestle that was used for making home remedies and for crushing herbs. Tables and dressers and other pieces of furniture from other times and locations occupy their places around the house. They each have their own story. My grandfather, a Swedish immigrant farmer, created some of the paintings, while some paintings are from the various travels of my parents. Scattered in different places you find pieces of African art brought to us by a friend who lived in Africa while her husband worked to control malaria. All these artifacts are familiar to me because I lived in that house and understand their origins and stories. In some way, these artifacts make up part of my experience of what "home" means. If, however, someone came to visit who didn't know the stories behind these artifacts, they would appear strange to him or her, or they would not convey meaning and connection to the past.

- Name some of the artifacts around your home or the home of a relative that contain a story or speak of who you are or your people and heritage.

  _____

  _____

When I visit churches and experience different worship services, styles, and traditions, I notice the artifacts present there as well. They are not always physical items like a Swedish Bible or a piece of African art, but the songs, prayers, architecture, and language all tell a story of origin. Different "artifacts" show up in our churches in a variety of ways. As we observe them, we can see the family resemblance passed to us from previous generations of worshipers. As you read the next section, imagine the ways in which these developments in worship style have shaped your church's current worship style and note your observations in the "family resemblance" sections.

The next leg of our journey through time will be through the development of several historical worship forms across the centuries. Along the way, we will discover that, in many ways, the various worship styles we practice today are really a convergence of interpretations, communication styles, and historical developments. Observing the nature of different worship forms will provide some common ground from which to discuss our process of worshiping today as well as the planning and development of our worship experiences.[6]

Worship in the early Church

The earliest picture we have of Christians gathering for worship comes from the book of Acts. Read the following passage and try to picture what the gathering was like.

They devoted themselves to the apostles' teaching and fellowship, to the breaking of bread and the prayers.

Awe came upon everyone, because many wonders and signs were being done by the apostles. All who believed were together and had all things in common; they would sell their possessions and goods and distribute the proceeds to all, as any had need. Day by day, as they spent much time together in the temple, they broke bread at home and ate their food with glad and generous hearts, praising God and having the goodwill of all the people. And day by day the Lord added to their number those who were being saved. (Acts 2:42-47)

The gathering was characterized by teaching, fellowship, breaking bread, prayer, miracles, sharing of possessions, praise, and growth. Note that these early Christians continued to worship in the temple as well. This is a simple picture of a new movement of followers of the risen Christ, gathered to share in their relationship with Christ and to share life together. As Christianity grew and spread to other areas, it began to develop forms of worship that were separate from the temple. They organized in house churches, and fellowship and love played a big part in their life together. As they worshiped, probably gathered in a simple living room of someone's home, they read from scrolls and letters from the teaching of the apostles and the accounts of the life of Christ. They shared prayers of intercession for the members of the community and the world beyond. They shared in the sacrament of the bread and the cup as they recounted the story that Jesus had told his followers to remember. And as they prepared to depart, they took up offerings to be shared with the poor and members of the community who were facing hardship.

I can imagine Christians worshiping in a catacomb in ancient Rome, under threat of persecution or death if they were discovered, as they sat amidst death, dirt, and dust. They might have lifted voices in prayer and song, proclaiming the reality of their faith—that there is hope in the middle of brokenness and pain because God cared enough to enter their lives, to become incarnate in this temporal world.

• Family Resemblance:

_____

_____

Worship in the
Eastern Orthodox tradition

Three centuries later, as the Christian religion became more for-
malized and organized, it took on more dramatic and elaborate
forms. In the Eastern Orthodox expression of Christianity centered
in Byzantium, worship developed a highly symbolic and image-rich
form. Everything about the service, including the architecture of the
churches, contained symbols that told the story of their understanding of God's activity in the world and the heavenly realm. Elaborate
icons (illuminated dimensional paintings) were used to help illiter-
ate people understand and engage in the story. As people watched the
drama of worship unfold, and as they meditated on the images in the
icons and in the great domed ceiling painted to help them envision
God's rule over all the earth, they drew near to the story, offered
praise to God, and grew in their connection to the faith. The form of
worship itself was designed to imitate, as closely as possible, the picture of heavenly worship found in Revelation 4-5.

• Family Resemblance:

_____

_____

Worship in the early
Roman Catholic tradition

The Roman catholic church, (the western arm of the church centered in Rome) likewise developed a service of worship that was highly
symbolic and dramatic in nature. By the Middle Ages, worship had
become highly ritualized. The congregation attended as observers of
the unfolding drama performed by priests. Each word spoken (in
Latin, which was not the common language of the people), each action
performed, the crossing of oneself, the swinging of the incense, the
lifting of the bread, were filled with symbolism, most of which was
unknown to the congregation. In theory, through their activity in this
divine drama on earth, they were participating again in the act of God's
salvation through Christ's sacrifice. They were allowing God's grace to
be mediated through sacred ritual. The host (bread) was believed to
undergo a miraculous transformation and actually become the body of
Christ. Many believed that by simply gazing upon the bread, one
would receive grace and forgiveness.

- Family Resemblance:

_____

_____

Worship under the influence of the Reformation

The Reformation in the sixteenth century carried with it an attempt to purify worship from the layers of ritual and what the reformers considered unnecessary mystical trappings that were clouding the act of worship. Reformers wanted to return to the centrality of the proclamation of God's word in the language of the people. This reformed purification, while well intentioned, was responsible for the destruction of a great amount of historic, beautiful, scared art. "Reformers" destroyed the art because they claimed that people were worshiping the symbols as idols and were thus engaged in blasphemy.

The Reformation was unified in purpose but not in practice. Three different emphases in worship emerged. All of the Reformation churches developed worship in the language of the people and put a greater emphasis on the Word and the involvement of the congregation in worship. Some maintained many of the ancient rituals, while others tried to break completely from what they considered to be perversions of authentic scriptural worship. The architecture of these extreme churches removed any semblance of symbol and insisted on buildings that were plain and practical.

- Family Resemblance:

_____

_____

Worship forms in the Protestant Free Church

From the seventeenth through the nineteenth centuries, the Protestant Free Church tradition emerged. This movement continued the emphasis on the centrality of the Word in worship, but over time this emphasis moved in two distinct directions. One movement developed worship around a teaching model. The sermons were designed to educate and engage the congregation in discussion. Congregational questioning and feedback was encouraged. The purpose of the service was to continue the process of Christian formation through the development of knowledge and understanding. Later on, a new form of worship emerged that focused on conversion through dramatic oration that evoked an emotional response from the congregation. This form of worship was much less participative and much more presentational. It was at this point that the pulpit was commonly moved to the center of the chancel and elevated above the congregation on a platform. The earlier form of Protestant Free Church worship was educational, while the later form was evangelistic.

• Family Resemblance:

_____

_____

Worship in the early African-American experience

While these changes were going on in predominantly European and Euro-American churches, there was another form of worship developing among African-Americans who were still enslaved. Slaves were expected to participate in the churches of their owners. While many of the slaves had heard the gospel and had converted to Christianity, worshiping in the style and system of their owners was not appealing or helpful to them. It was not appealing partly because the musical style was foreign, but much more than that, the theology of the slave-owner churches promoted the idea that slaves were lesser human beings than their owners and encouraged the continuation of the institution of slavery.

Through great risk, ingenuity, and commitment, the slaves developed their own worship style and their own hymns. Those who were owned as slaves had to gather secretly to worship. If they were caught, they were punished severely because it was assumed that they were plotting against their masters. Their worship was emotionally charged and participational. They came to encounter the living Jesus, who understood pain and oppression and could connect them to a hope beyond and a greater alternative reality through worship. Sermons were rhythmic and centered in storytelling. The primary biblical stories had to do with God's power to redeem those being oppressed and the hope that was offered those who suffered. I can imagine how important, powerful, and transforming this secret act of worship was. It was an act that brought hope. It was an act through which they entered into a separate Kingdom reality, in which they were the valuable children of God they knew themselves to be.

• Family Resemblance:

_____

_____

Worship in the
Pentecostal/Holiness tradition

In the years following the Methodist expansion into North America, driven by primarily uneducated Methodist and other circuit-riding ministers who had experienced conversion and felt called to the ministry, a new form of worship began to spring up on the American frontier. Camp meetings were revival-like gatherings of people who were isolated and tried by the difficulties of frontier living, people who longed (as did the slaves) for a hope and a promise that was greater than the struggles of their everyday lives. These meetings were prolonged, emotionally-charged gatherings, characterized by passionate gospel singing, personal conversion, and with an emphasis on the experience of the baptism of the Spirit. From this form of intense, emotional, evangelical and sometimes ecstatic worship emerged the Pentecostal worship tradition. Pentecostal worship is characterized by a focus on the Holy Spirit. Pentecostalism grew into many forms over the next couple of centuries, including the Salvation Army. Among worship movements that emerged to a great extent from the Pentecostal tradition are charismatic worship and the praise and worship movement.

• Family Resemblance:

_____

_____

Worship in the Contemporary
Liturgical Renewal movement

In the late 1960s, the Roman Catholic Church released a document (from a conference called Vatican II) containing reforms of the church's liturgy. This major shift in Catholic liturgy reemphasized the ministry of the Word, and the importance of holding Mass in the common language of the people, rather than in Latin. Along with these liturgical reforms, Catholics reemphasized the depth of their commitment to their ancient liturgical practices and the centrality of the sacraments. This report was much too complex to explore in this brief overview, but the effects of this reform within the Catholic community were felt in mainline

Protestant churches that reviewed the documents carefully and applied what they learned to the renewal of their own liturgical practices.

This series of events birthed what has come to be known as the contemporary liturgical renewal. Protestants began to seriously consider again the liturgical roots of worship. Denominations issued new books of worship containing renewed liturgical forms for use in local congregations. To varying degrees, they were adopted in churches across the nation. Churches participating in the contemporary liturgical renewal movement affirm centrality of the Scripture in teaching and worship, understand and incorporate the rhythms of the liturgical year, demonstrate ecumenical concern, and emphasize the importance of the Eucharist (Holy Communion).

- Family Resemblance:

_____

_____

Worship in the Charismatic and Praise movements

The Charismatic and praise and worship movements were closely linked. Both emerged from Pentecostal worship forms. The Charismatic movement began as a prayer movement in the 1960s and emphasized the gifts of the Spirit in worship, which included prophecy, healing, and speaking in tongues. The Charismatic movement did not develop into one particular worship format, but emerged in churches of many types. Central to Charismatic worship is the presence and manifestation of the activities of the Holy Spirit.

The term "praise and worship" has come to be synonymous with particular types of worship choruses used in what many people refer to as "contemporary" worship. Some traditionalists joke unfairly about this type of music, calling it "7-11 worship." (Sing the same seven words eleven times.) However, many people don't know there is a scriptural reason that the praise and worship movement came into being. The concept of praise as a precursor to worship can be found in both the Old and New testaments. The praise and worship movement that started during the 1960s and 1970s emphasizes praise as an invocation of the presence of God and as a precedent to worship. God becomes "enthroned" on the praises of God's people. After praise is lifted, God's presence is encountered, and worship can begin.

• Family Resemblance:

_____

_____

Worship in a Seeker service

Seeker worship became popular with the advent of the church growth movement. Worship services were designed to be attractive, non-threatening events to which Christians could bring non-Christian friends where they could be exposed to a presentation of the gospel. Willow Creek (a congregation in the northwest suburbs of Chicago) championed this style of worship. The services and worship area were stripped of "religious" symbols and language in an attempt to remove barriers that could stand in the way of people hearing the gospel. Pure seeker services are focused more on evangelistic presentation (through drama, teaching, and imagery) than the activity of worship.

In a society with so much rapid and progressive change, it is not surprising that these influences are converging into new resemblances. Junius Dotson, senior pastor of St. Mark's United Methodist Church in Wichita, Kansas describes "neo-pentecostalism." He reports that this is one of the fastest growing forms of worship, especially in larger urban African-American congregations. Neo-Pentecostalism is an emerging form of worship that has roots and patterns in the past; Rev. Dotson described a service that was high-energy, educated, liturgically influenced, Spirit-filled, evangelical and musically eclectic.

Cultural diversity and multiculturalism are becoming more prevalent all across the nation. Services exist to provide worship for people of many cultures in native style and language. Many congregations know the experience of having children grow up influenced more by the contemporary culture than the traditions and cultures of their parents. Questions arise as to how to sustain the worship traditions and styles that have been handed down from generation to generation. Other questions arise as individuals and congregations from different cultural backgrounds try to worship together without losing cultural identity.

• Family Resemblance:

_____

_____

Stop for a moment and think about all the change and transition that has been going on over the years and is still going on all around us. Do you think there were any moments of conflict about these different worship styles among people who worshiped during the periods of change and transition? And perhaps more importantly, would it be possible for a congregation to incorporate elements from two or more of these worship styles and still be worshiping faithfully in the Christian tradition?

A new, old thing?

The services of Willow Creek, and many of those who follow the "seeker" format, have discovered that newer generations do not want a service that is distant, removed, and designed only for viewing. They are looking for an experience that engages them heart, mind, and soul. From the mid-1990s Ginghamsburg United Methodist Church in Ohio and Willow Creek bare influenced tens of thousands of churches to increase the use of the arts, visuals, musical and dramatic, in its services. More traditional churches, as well, are attempting to merge different elements of expression into existing worship styles. Some congregations are adding screens as a supplement to the printed bulletin, or to help illustrate points in a sermon. Many of these churches are also making more use of the arts in worship. Churches, young and old who, are discovering a revitalization, a renewing, or what I would refer to as a reconnecting in worship.

Tom Long observes, "These churches have created a new thing in the earth, a form of worship that is authentically Christian, theologically rich and magnetic to a seeking, restless, individualistic, de-institutionalized culture." These "vital and faithful" congregations:

- make room in worship for the experience of mystery,
- make efforts to show hospitality to the stranger,
- make visible the sense of drama in Christian worship,
- emphasize music that is both excellent and eclectic,
- creatively adapt the worship space and environment,
- forge a strong connection between worship and local mission,
- maintain a relatively stable order of service that the congregation knows by heart,
- move to a joyous, festive experience near the end of the service.[7]

As I look at various worship traditions, I see elements in each that are appealing to me. I also have seen many of them incorporated in worship services I have attended.

We are entering a period of a convergence among worship traditions. As we look at the images of our Christian ancestors through their expressions of worship, we see that they do not all look alike, but there is a family resemblance. Robert Webber (of Wheaton College) reports that the family resemblance can be seen in an emphasis on 1) the importance of the sacraments; 2) desire to understand the early church; 3) love for the whole Church, universal; 4) a mix of structure and spontaneity; 5) the use of sign and symbol; 6) personal salvation and bible teaching; and 7) the work and ministry of the Holy Spirit.[8]

God seems to be doing a new thing, but more like a new old thing; not producing a replica of an antique but remembering how to create beautiful jewelry by silver smithing, keeping the patterns and the purity of the metal and using new ways to bring that beauty to expression.

Some people assume that worship has remained basically unchanged across the centuries and that the changes being brought forth in worship today are an affront to the changeless nature of worship. As you can see from our journey through the different changes in the church, as well as sources and forms of worship, change has been as much a part of the history of the Church as people. As we examine the different currents of worship, we can see that most of them have emerged from passionate and convicted Christians who are struggling to be faithful in their given tradition, in their specific cultural and historical setting and to their deeply held convictions. As we look at the different expressions of worship—some ancient, some old, and some relatively new—is there a clear answer to common questions: "Which one is right?" "Which one is traditional?"

We can learn much from the old pictures in the scrapbook of our shared history and from the stories and artifacts that come to us from previous generations. If we step back and look deeper at the things that shape our experience as congregations and our varied worship styles, we may be surprised at the family resemblance we are able to see.

The reality of change and evolution in the forms of worship is undeniable. Something not divorced from the past, yet a new creation, is emerging, being born, taking form. The need to focus is not simply on the form worship takes, but on the continuity of the grace and love of God that is mediated through congregational worship. In the next chapter we will consider to learn how to worship faithfully, where tradition and innovation converge.

Chapter Three Connections

Planting

As you think about your congregation in the future, what artifacts do you imagine as part of your congregation's history?

In completing the Gifts exercise this week, allow "your service" to be explained as you envision it five years from now.

In the Service exercise this week, say thank you to a person who plays a supportive role in the process of the new church start.

Prayer

Pray for those who will provide leadership in your worship service this week. Remember them as they prepare during the week.

Presence

This week, when you walk around your church facility, or while you attend worship, look for "artifacts" that may tell a story. They might be a particular prayer that is corporately prayed, a piece of stained glass, or the placement of the pulpit. Notice the way your worship space is arranged. Listen, observe, and reflect on the ways in which these "artifacts" have shaped your congregation's current worship style. Make a list of the items you discover in your journal. Note how they affect your personal worship experience.

Gifts

In yur journal, write a letter explaining your worship service to a person who has never attended; it may be a relative, a coworker, a friend, or a spouse. If possible, think of someone who is not a regular worship attendee of any congregation. Do not write the letter from an evangelistic approach. (Don't write why they *need* to be in church.) Instead, be descriptive. What style do you use? Why do you worship? Share what the service means to you and how you are affected by the experience. Use the letter to identify your own personal "why" for worship discussed in Session Two. Why do you worship, and why is it important to you?

Service

Identify someone in your congregation who participates in the worship service each week whom you do not physically "see." It could be the person who vacuums the worship area, one who folds the bulletins, one who prays with the prayer team for the service before worship, or one who works in the nursery during the service. Whoever it is, find a way to say thank you to that person this week. It might be with words, a card, or a special gift. In some way, acknowledge another individual to indicate that what he or she does makes a difference in the life of worship for your congregation.

Consider how you might aid in the worship preparation process of your congregation. Is there something you might do to be helpful in one of the supportive roles of worship?

'e' ventures

This week, spend some time at www.methodx.net. In this digital age, how is spirituality and community connecting with emerging generations? Explore this site and notice how you "connect" to the experience. Take the "spiritual types test" and identify your spiritual type. Check out the community and spiritual practices section. Other similar websites to explore:

www.jesuit.ie/prayer/, www.ginkworld.net, and www.beliefnet.com.

Session Three Video

The video segment on the DVD or VHS in the *ReConnecting Worship Kit* that corresponds to this chapter is Session Three: *Cultural Archaeology and Emerging Worship.*

Chapter Four
Where Tradition and
Innovation Converge

We've seen the tension present in real churches. We have explored the "why" of worship. We have taken a journey through some of the old family photos and toured the artifacts of previous generations responding to change. Change is a reality of life. In this chapter, we turn our attention to the heart of the matter—the intersection between faithfulness to the purposes of worship found in the traditions of our ancestors, and the process of innovation that is required to sustain the purposes of worship in a rapidly and radically changing world.

Change is necessary
for living things.

Some people might ask, "With all this tradition available to us, is innovation ever allowable or necessary?" Perhaps this is the wrong way to approach the issue. Consider the nature of change itself.

It was a warm and sunny spring day in Mississippi. Inside the red brick building on the campus of the college, we sat at old desks and listened to the professor discuss the nature of change and permanence. "Twenty years from now, will you be the same people you are now?" The question seemed somewhat strange, especially because most of us had not yet experienced what it meant to live twenty years.

"Of course we will be the same people," said one of the students.

"Will you?" asked the professor, the raised pitch of the words inviting us to ponder the issue.

He went on to talk about the rate at which the human body replaces cells, and that approximately every eighteen months the body completely replaces itself. He spoke of the change in roles that would be experienced, from student to professional and from child to parent. He spoke about changed surroundings and demands. He suggested that the nature of our experience and concerns would be different. If all of these things change—physical bodies, experiences, roles, surroundings, responsibilities and daily activities—are we indeed the same people? Of course we are the same people. We may have different cells. We may be different sizes. We may have more or less hair, but we are the same people. We are the same, while we have changed. There is a thread of spirit, memory, purpose, and identity that binds us throughout time and through changing locations and experiences.

Twenty years have passed and now I apply the line of reasoning to the liturgical life of the Church. Like the human body and human life itself, the Church is a living body. Its cells (people) are replaced as the years pass. The Church's surroundings and concerns change, as do its forms, liturgies, and practices. Over time, the shape and style of our expression may change, yet we remain the same if we are faithful to the spirit, memory, purpose, and identity of our heritage.

Is innovation (change) acceptable? I would answer that *change happens*. It is part of life. Our responsibility is to participate in faithfully shaping it and allowing it to shape us where needed.

Change will cause a certain degree of discomfort. The emergence of forms of worship has engendered a crisis of sorts in the lives of many mainline churches. It is not surprising that the response to the challenge posed by these new worship forms has been divisiveness, blaming, and scrambling for control of turf. As we noted in the previous chapter, the issue of diversity of worship styles, however, is not a new one. Across the years, churches embraced a variety of worship styles within varied congregations. Congregations worship in differing formats, such as Southern gospel, high church, camp meeting, African-American spiritual, to name a few. Official books of worship and denominational hymnals have included liturgies and rituals from diverse cultural groups and hymns in languages other than English. Diversity has been valued in the past, and the practice of the adaptation of worship forms to cultural settings extends in the various traditions as well. Why, then, are new forms of cultural adaptation causing problems?

If successive generations cease to respond to the musical and communication styles used in our worship services and, thus, seek spiritual nurture and fulfillment elsewhere, then worship is no longer able to accomplish its task of building and developing successive generations whose lives are shaped and enriched by the story of God. Sadly, in many congregations, that future is already here, and the doors of these churches are closing. How do we respond to this situation? One strain of thought is that mainline churches should adopt practices that would make the church more attractive to younger generations. This approach raises a number of questions. Should the current service be altered? Should the old forms be cast aside? Should the church add an additional service with an alternative style to reach younger generations? Should the church adapt to the changes in culture at all? All of these questions are potentially divisive and conflicting.

The changes in younger generations' tastes in music, orientation toward informality, conversance with electronic media, and the phenomenon of dislocation from tradition have brought cultural diversity within the walls of the existing community. It is much easier to tolerate and even to value diversity of style when it is practiced in the little country church "down the road" that will use only the "old time gospel" hymnal, or when the guitars are played at the youth gathering around a fire at camp. Youth who return home from such a gathering have experienced community building and connection to God's story, an encounter with the sacred mediated by the music within their cultural idiom, and it is usually acceptable for them to share a song in worship. What if, however, the youth want a different style of music as part of corporate worship on a regular basis? Is it time for them to leave and start a new church? Should they get over their desire to express thanksgiving to God in a familiar and heartfelt style and learn the music that *others* prefer? A powerful point of tension comes when the diversity is not separated by individual community boundaries, but exists within the congregation's own life. The possibility of the need for change frequently threatens a congregation's sense of continuity and stability and thus evokes a reactive response.

Reaction to change

Many leaders approach the issue of liturgical continuity and the faithful response to change as if it were a new issue. However, the struggle of faithfulness to tradition in the face of constantly changing life is an old one. As the currents of social, cultural, language, and technological change swirl around us, different voices emerge in response. Some voices are revolutionary. Some are reactive.

When computers first started to emerge as tools for home and office use, some people reacted strongly. "I don't do computers," they would say. "They are a waste of money and time." Now, with computers a major part of daily life, many of those who voiced opposition to computers are now adept at sharing photos, documents, and messages through email, word processing, surfing the web for information, and shopping or banking online.

In such times, the guiding question must not be narcissistic (what do I like?), but rather pragmatic (what will best accomplish our purpose?). Leonard Sweet observes, "The issue for us today is not whether the gospel will be inculturated in this electronic age, but how; not whether our social context shapes our experience of the gospel, but how."

As I write this paragraph, I am in a cabin on a lake in rural Louisiana. It is a comfortable, yet rustic, place of retreat shared with me by a friend and member of the congregation I serve. I often spend one day and night here a week to pray and write. Recently, my friend has been doing some renovations to the camp house that will make it much nicer in the long run. The process of change causes some inconveniences and disruptions in the schedule. If, however, I would rather not fall through the shower floor into the lake below, I will adapt to the process of change and look toward the ultimate benefits of the present inconvenience. Change is natural and sometimes uncomfortable, but it can have great benefits.

Neither change nor the resistance to change is faithful or good in and of itself. I have experienced contemporary worship and traditional worship that were faithful to the task of building the community of people by orienting them to God. I have also experienced worship, both contemporary and traditional, that failed at this task. When those who design worship in either style miss the focus of building community by failing to orient people toward God and grounding them in the Story, they are not being faithful.

Sometimes changes are made that adapt to culture without the purpose of or possibility for transformation of the culture through the power of the gospel. I was living in Denver, Colorado, during one of the years that the Broncos made it to the Super Bowl. The people in Denver went crazy, as do other communities when their teams do well. Orange was everywhere. People wore orange, painted their faces orange, and drank Orange Crush (the nickname for the Broncos' defensive team). As "Broncomania" swept the city, it entered the church in a way that was inappropriate. One well-meaning seamstress created something for the pastor of the church—as much for a joke as anything else—an orange stole with a Broncos insignia. I don't know if she intended for him to wear it, but he did—for corporate worship. Swept up in the cultural phenomenon of "Broncomania," other members of the church took this cultural adaptation one step further and used Orange Crush instead of grape juice during communion. While the intent of this activity was not malicious, it was disturbing to me and to many members of the congregation (who were loyal Broncos fans) because it was an accommodation of the culture that cheapened the sacrament. While engaging some people and building excitement, it was misdirected, making a cultural phenomenon the center of sacred activity rather than allowing the sacred activity to inform and transform the culture. This example is admittedly extreme, but it demonstrates the nature of change that accommodates the culture in a negative way.

Resistance to change in extreme forms is not always the faithful response either. Sometimes tradition resists adaptation to language and culture to the point that it cannot leaven the society it is called to transform. Sometimes changes surrounding the church involve new groups of people who are different from those inside the congregation. Sometimes the changes have to do with the aging of the congregation and the lack of intentional efforts to develop methods that will attract and involve younger generations. Sometimes the change is in styles of communication and musical expression that engage the hearts and minds of those outside the church. If a church remains an island unto itself, without concern for those in the surrounding community, it will be destined for decline, ineffectiveness, and ultimately, death. I have witnessed this scenario at an increasing pace in many churches, and for many more the handwriting is on the wall. The real issue is how churches respond to the reality of change and maintain openness to one another as we seek to respond to those changes and move faithfully forward.

One of the great philosophers, social commentators, and children's authors of this century, Dr. Seuss wrote a book entitled *The Butter Battle Book*. The story is about two tribes of very similar creatures who are in conflict. The center of their conflict is the proper way to butter bread. One tribe butters the bread with the butter side up. The other tribe butters the bread with the butter side down. This conflict escalates to the point that the two tribes are at war and design successively more destructive weapons to attack each other. The story is a parody of the human tendency to defend one particular practice with great tenacity and to attack those who are different, even if the difference is ultimately insignificant. Many of the struggles within the Christian community surrounding the nature of worship are similar to the scenario described

by Dr. Seuss. There are important issues of faithfulness to be considered, but in many ways we are spending our energy attacking our own
people instead of working together to bring God's story to a hurting and
broken world.

The glut of information on both sides of the argument, while effectively raising important questions, is serving to tear the Body of Christ
apart. Marva Dawn, in *Reaching Out Without Dumbing Down*, provides
support for the motivations of both sides of what has been termed the
"worship wars," as well as direction for planners and leaders of worship.
She clearly states the nature of the tension, calling attention to the validity of the positions of both parties.

> Enthusiasts for contemporary worship are right in seeking to
> reach out to persons in the culture around us and in rejecting tra-
> dition that has grown stale. Those who value the Church's worship
> heritage are right to question the faithfulness and integrity of
> many contemporary worship forms and to seek a noticeable dif-
> ference in worship that underscores the Church's countercultural
> emphasis. Only in a dialectical tension of tradition and reforma-
> tion can we ask better questions to ensure that worship is consis-
> tent with the nature of God as revealed in the Scriptures and in the
> person of Jesus Christ.[9]

It is between the two poles of this tension that the church finds its
point of conflict, and it is in this tension that the church will find its
ability to move faithfully with integrity into the future.

Part of the dynamic of the resistance to change is found in
Contemporary Worship for the 21st Century. The authors make an important distinction among three words with the same root, yet with very
different meanings and implications for the church: tradition, traditional, and traditionalism.

Tradition—a good word meaning "the living faith of the dead." The
tradition is the embodiment of the Christian faith as contained in the
Scriptures through the belief and practice of the disciples through the
centuries and handed on to present and future generations.

Traditional—a congregation or denomination's familiar practices
rooted in a given era. What is traditional usually reflects a particular
innovation that was embraced in the light of the sensibilities and realities of a particular time and place. When the culture changes, the

traditional practice may need to be transformed or discarded in order for the living faith of the tradition to move forward.

Traditionalism—a sad reality: "the dead faith of the living." When faith is encapsulated in particular forms, words and routines without the vitality of vision, and the Holy Spirit's transforming power, the deadly result is traditionalism.[10]

Congregations in which the tradition of the church is engaged in life-giving, life-affirming, challenging and renewing ways have worship that is alive and dynamic. Other congregations use particular forms simply because that is what has always been done before.

• Can you think of an example of these two situations?

_____

_____

_____

There is no doubt that we love our worship, and that we have become comfortable with and attached to particular expressions and forms of worship. We like to imagine things we love as changeless; the trick is to learn to love the changeless in the midst of change. We must determine what is essential to our tradition and what is simply something we embrace because we don't know what else to do. Likewise, we must examine new forms of worship that are introduced and see if they meet the standard of carrying the tradition and orienting people toward God. We explore some of these standards later in this chapter.

A point of contention

Several complaints about contemporary worship arise frequently: (1) It is performance-oriented and, therefore, places the focus on the leader rather than on God; (2) It is shallow in content, as it always tries to present a message that is upbeat and happy; (3) It uses entertainment methods simply to draw a crowd at the expense of the gospel and the building of the community of the cross. All of these criticisms have proven true in certain situations, yet to caricature all worship that uses elements of contemporary methods of expression as happy, shallow showmanship designed to draw a crowd without regard to the message of the gospel is wrong. It is just as wrong to caricature all traditional, classically oriented worship as dry, dead, outdated examples of museum-maintaining intellectual and cultural elitism. It is important to remember that while the form of worship can aid in its ability to accomplish its purpose, ultimately, the medium is not the message. The message can be conveyed in a variety of ways.

Some people ask, "Is there any value in the new forms of worship that are emerging, or are they just styles used to draw a crowd?" One answer can be found in the research and writing of a religion professor who set out on a project to analyze new-style churches with an admitted bias against the new forms. As a result of five years of research and hundreds of interviews in what he terms "new paradigm" churches, Donald Miller, professor of religion, released an important book entitled *Reinventing American Protestantism*. In his study, he concludes that the phenomenon known as the new paradigm church is an effective form of American Christianity and that churches had developed ways to engage people in a transforming, community-building, life-giving relationship with God. At first skeptical, Miller became convinced through interviews with pastors, church leaders, and lay members that these churches are not "selling out" to contemporary society. They are "doing a better job at responding to the needs of their clientele than are many mainline churches, but—more importantly—they are successfully mediating the sacred, bringing God to people and conveying the self-transcending and life-changing core of all true religion."[11]

Change can be good or bad. As we work to develop meaningful and effective worship experiences, the most important question is, "How can healthy tradition guide effective and faithful innovation?" Tradition and innovation seem to some people to be mutually exclusive. *The place of intersection evokes images of conflict and "choosing sides." I agree that there is a tension where tradition and innovation meet and I suppose there always will be. Perhaps surprisingly, I believe that this can be a good thing.*

Here's the rub.

Tension can cause friction. Sometimes friction causes pain, as when skin scrapes across concrete when a child falls on the sidewalk. Sometimes friction can cause excessive and damaging heat, as when we forget to check the oil in the car and the engine burns up. These experiences of friction are destructive and unpleasant. Some friction, however, is helpful, such as the friction that enables a match to strike and in turn ignite a fire to bring warmth to the house, or the friction that enables brakes to stop a car so it doesn't run into a tree. While the discussion surrounding tradition and innovation has caused quite a lot of heat, and in some places no small amount of pain, I like to think of the tension between these two realities in a constructive light. To continue with the transportation analogy, consider another innovative approach to the challenges presented by an oil-based transportation industry.

Recently, carmakers, including Toyota, Honda and Ford, have developed technology based partially on oil and partially on a previously unrecognized and untapped source of energy. In the past, the only energy considered important in a car was the energy that caused it to be propelled and to run the internal systems such as the radio, lights, and climate control. Petroleum-based engines provided the energy to propel the car while generators connected to the engine supported the other systems. The engineers of these new vehicles looked at the car from a different perspective and found another source of energy that could be harnessed without additional fuel consumption: the brakes. Brakes, when applied, engage a force that reduces the forward momentum of the vehicle. As the brakes are applied, a great deal of friction is created. Friction creates energy, most often experienced as heat. For example, as when driving down mountains, brakes used to keep the car from careening off the side of the mountain create heat. Engineers looked at this friction as a potential source of energy that, if captured, could be used to propel the car and power its internal systems.

Engineers designed a system of generators to transfer the friction and momentum energy into electricity. The electricity generated is stored in large batteries and used to run an electric engine that can either complement or replace the gas engine. In many cases, when used to supplement the gas engine, this use of alternative energy has increased fuel efficiency by more than 100 percent.

Imagine if we had known to capture all of energy from all the braking since the advent of the automobile. That is a lot of energy. As hybrid cars improve and become the norm (perhaps even combining hydrogen fuel cells with hybrid technology), consider how much farther cars will be propelled because some carmakers chose to look at tension in a new way. The tension we experience in the worshiping community might provide a similar energy if we can choose to look at it creatively and harness it, rather than simply allowing it to create heat and smoke. As Marva Dawn states, "Only in a *dialectical tension of tradition and reformation* can we ask better questions to ensure that worship is consistent with the nature of God as revealed in the Scriptures and in the person of Jesus Christ."[12]

What are the standards that harness this tension for the purpose of faithful innovation?

Standard One: Elements of structure

The first standard concerns understanding the elements of worship. Innovation must be sensitive to continuity in pattern and purpose. Liturgical traditions provide continuity of expression and content to our worship experiences over time and from place to place. The pattern of worship is given to us over centuries of worship practice in the Christian community. The elements of the worship experience are given to us as gathering, prayer, adoration, proclamation, response, confession, thanksgiving, and sending forth.

Let's examine each of these elements briefly.

Gathering

The gathering of God's people is an important element of worship in that it is a reminder of why we come together. Recognition of the unique nature of the assembly helps to reconnect those who are part of the community with the reason for their participation, and to inform guests about the purpose of worship. Think about a wedding. When the minister stands to begin the ceremony, he or she says, "We have gathered today to witness the joining together of Sarah and Melvin in Christian marriage." Well, some might say, "That is as obvious as the nose on your face. I got the invitation, and it said 'Wedding.' I see the man in the tux and the woman in the big white dress; what else would we be doing here?" In stating the reason, those in attendance are reminded that this is not simply a social event, or the precursor to a reception, but an assembly in the context of a faith story, and in the presence of God. It stretches back across the ages. This act of gathering serves the same purpose in all services of worship.

Prayer

As we gather together in the presence of God, we are called to enter into relationship with God. We do not gather simply to witness an event, to fulfill a social obligation, or to be entertained or encouraged. We gather as a community with the God who has given us life and continually calls us to gather and be shaped in God's image. Some modern expressions of worship have attempted to jettison many of the acts and symbols of the church in order to make the service more familiar to those outside the community of faith. At times, some churches have removed the activity of prayer from worship. This is an ineffective approach. In my experience, as those outside the church community witness the reality of people in communication with God, they will be inspired to seek a similar relationship. Use of prayers such as the Lord's Prayer can provide an opportunity for the introduction of prayer to newcomers as well as a familiar rhythm of faith for members. Prayers such as the Lord's Prayer are often memorized by members, but need to be printed in the bulletin, projected on the screen, or otherwise made readily available to guests.

Adoration

Adoration is the act of expressing love for God. Remember the definition of worship—ascribing to God the place of ultimate value in life. This is the activity of adoration. Adoration can take many forms. It can be expressed in hymns and choruses of praise. It can be spoken corporately. It can be expressed silently, symbolically, or through a variety of other creative methods. We gather to offer God our worship and to express our love.

Proclamation

Proclamation is centered in the Scripture and presents the Word of God as the source of the community's direction, identity, and reason for being. Proclamation of the Word of God lifts before the community a reminder of the higher calling of the Christian community to love the Lord with all our heart, mind, soul, and strength, and to love our neighbors as ourselves. Through proclamation, Christians receive the message of God, interpreted through the lens of current reality, and encourage, correct, heal, challenge, and nourish for a life of faithful discipleship.

Response

Worship is not a passive experience for the congregation. God's activity, presence, and message call for the response of the people. God's activity always precedes our response. The term "seekers" can be misleading because it might imply that God is inactive until people find God. The opposite is true. It is God who is actively seeking us. Our response can take many forms. Sometimes the response is for new or renewed commitment to the life of discipleship. Sometimes the response is to offer our resources so the work of God can be shared through and beyond the congregation. Sometimes the response is to forgive others as we ourselves have been forgiven. It is the expectation of and the call for response that remind the congregation of the transforming power of God in and through the lives of the gathered people.

Confession

The act of confession reminds us of our tendency to stray from the ways of God. People are good at rationalizing destructive and selfish behaviors, and are capable of imagining that they are above the need for God's forgiveness. Confession isn't meant to be a "guilt trip" that leaves the participants focused on their imperfection. Rather, it is a reminder that while all of us are broken and sinful in places, as we are honest with God, our brokenness is made whole and our sinfulness is forgiven. "If we confess our sins, God is faithful and just and will forgive our sins and free us from all unrighteousness." (1 John 1:9) The act of confession is the seeking of freedom and an opportunity to engage life refreshed, renewed, and remade.

Thanksgiving

In worship we are reminded that God is the source of our life. God is the giver of all good gifts, including the gift of salvation through Jesus Christ and the sustaining presence of the Holy Spirit. The act of thanksgiving is the corporate response to that reality. As we express thanks to God for life, we are reminded that it is by grace that we live and that our entire lives become an act of thankful response to the Creator.

Sending Forth

At the end of a class, the bell rings and it is time to leave because the allotted time for that subject has ended. When we reach the end of a counseling session, the therapist says, "Well, that's all the time we have for today." A worship service doesn't conclude in the same way because the activity of worship is not an end in itself. The worshiping community exists for the transformation of the world. The intentional act of sending forth is a reminder that the transition into the world is the continuation of our living response to God's gracious activity and that God's presence in the world around us both precedes and calls us to participate in a life of ministry.

These elements constitute our pattern for communal worship. They will not always look the same, but they should be accounted for in the flow of the service. It is necessary to determine what changeless spirit and memory must be maintained, and then, faithfully articulate it in ways that are meaningful to each time and situation. It is in the dynamic tension between tradition and creative innovation that we find the energy needed for faithful, relevant, and transformational worship experiences. Patterns can be cut out of a variety of cloth and adapted to suit culture, climate, and condition.

Standard Two: Theology of the presence and activity of God

The second standard has to do with the multifaceted presence of God expressed through worship. If we are to be faithful to the tradition and purpose of worship, then it is not as much a question of which liturgy or music we will use as to how we effectively mediate of the multifaceted presence and activity of God. One way to describe this multifaceted activity of God is through the term the *order of salvation*.

Theodore Weber writes, "The heart of John Wesley's evangelism is the message that God acts to restore the lost moral image, not for the few, but for the entire human race; not coercively, but through the empowerment of the Holy Spirit that enables the response to God's gracious gift. God opens our eyes to our condition of being without God in the world (prevenient grace), bestows forgiveness of sins (justifying grace), and encourages us lovingly to become more loving and to "have that mind which also was in Christ Jesus" (sanctifying grace, Christian perfection). Through this process, this grace-filled ordering of salvation, the moral image is restored, the "capacity for God" returns, true humanity is recovered, and the born-again creature comes to stand before God and to love other creatures in the holiness of grace. This is the good news, the evangelical tidings for lost sinners and for the rest of creation damaged through their sinning. It is the order of God's salvation for sinful humanity.[13]

The question for those involved in designing worship services that are faithful to tradition, no matter what style is used, becomes one of presenting the *order of salvation* clearly for those who participate. Are the voices of prevenient, justifying, and sanctifying grace woven into an experience that calls people into the ongoing process of God's redemptive work in creation?

1. Does the form of our worship expression recognize and articulate the grace of God that is universally available and draws us toward repentance (prevenient grace)?
2. Do our services call people to the reality of transformation and rebirth through the justifying grace of God (justifying grace)?

3. Do our services provide a setting for response to these first
two movements in thanksgiving and encourage the living of
lives that continue to grow in grace and selfless servanthood
(sanctification)?

If these elements are not present, then it does not matter what the
style of the liturgy or what type of music or format is used; the continuity and integrity of our theological tradition is lacking.

We can find in the worship resources of our ancestors a library of
possibilities for the construction of worship services that are faithful to
our theological purpose and tradition. These, however, should be seen
as resources rather than restrictions. We are God's children, who share
God's creative genes and, likewise, have been given all creation as the
artist's palette for our worship of God.

Liturgical tradition is a beautiful, deep well of faith, heritage, and
theology, and it is a great source of life for us. The issue before us is how
are we to relate to this tradition as we move into a new and ever-changing present? In Joshua, we read of the twelve stones that were set up as
reminders to future generations so that people would never forget what
God had done in the lives of the people as they moved into a whole new
land.

Those twelve stones, which they had taken out of the Jordan,
Joshua set up in Gilgal, saying to the Israelites, "When your children ask their parents in time to come, 'What do these stones
mean?' then you shall let your children know, 'Israel crossed over
the Jordan here on dry ground.' For the Lord your God dried up
the waters of the Jordan for you until you crossed over, as the Lord
your God did to the Red Sea, which he dried up for us until we
crossed over, so that all the peoples of the earth may know that the
hand of the Lord is mighty, and so that you may fear the Lord your
God forever." (Joshua 4:20-24)

The stones *pointed* the people to sacred memory. The stones were
not, of themselves, sacred, but they pointed to the sacred. Our liturgy,
like these stones, serves to point toward the sacred—yet it is not the
liturgy that we worship. Ascribing sacred worth to the wrong thing can
become a big problem, as the Pharisees discovered when Jesus chastised
them about swearing by the gold on the Temple rather than the Temple
itself that made the gold sacred (Matthew 23:16-22).

Standard Three: Hospitality for the guest, the stranger, or the sojourner

The primary task of worship is to build community grounded in the Story and to orient people toward God. However, if left unspoken, the important dimension of hospitality could be neglected. Hospitality is concerned with welcoming the stranger and receiving the guest. It is a wonderful thing when a congregation has powerful and engaging worship that allows for community grounded in the Story of God and an encounter with God. But if the particular practices and the language of the worshiping community are strange or incomprehensible to those whom they are trying to reach, then the dimension of hospitality has been neglected. The language and style we use either takes into account the guest and the stranger, who can be one and the same, or it does not. The attitude of a church may be, "This works for me; they can take it or leave it," but that is hardly an attitude of hospitality. The standard of hospitality is applicable to new services and existing services. It is important in both traditional and contemporary formats. When considering the guest and the stranger, it may be necessary either to make the existing service more accessible to those who would come or to offer a different type of service.

Part of faithful innovation in light of the standard of hospitality requires our working to understand the "world" of those outside the church with whom we are called to share the gospel message. Dr. Andrew Sung Park of United Theological Seminary shared with me, "unless we understand other cultures, there is no way we can communicate the depth of the Christian gospel." This stands at the heart of the standard of hospitality.

What makes up your world? This may seem like a strange question, because we all live in the same physical world, the same planet, the same space and time universe, the same physical laws, the same earth, air, fire, and water. However, our world is not physical alone. It is composed of many different thoughts, stories, and experiences. Each person's world is a tapestry woven together with threads of language, story, cultural tradition, education, opportunity, fears, individual experiences, history, values, hopes, and dreams. My world is very different from the world of someone from a different cultural and social situation. If we are to be truly hospitable in the design of our worship services, we must become sensitive to the world in which those we are called to reach live. This is not easy. It requires stretching into unfamiliar places and developing relationships. It is not easy, but it is faithful. The standard of hospitality requires that we work to understand the world of those who would come, and design worship with a style of communication and expression that allows for open points of entry for the guest, the stranger, or the sojourner.

Let's take a moment to review what we have covered. Change is a reality, not a choice. Like the automakers, the designers of worship are faced with a decision to acknowledge the reality of change, adapt to it, or die. The energy for faithful change is found in the powerful and creative tension between tradition and innovation. There are elements of the structure, theology, and hospitality of worship that must be maintained. If congregations can agree to develop patterns of worship that effectively harness the tension rather than being reactive and inwardly divisive, then we can tap a source of power that will propel us faithfully into the future.

Reconnecting in worship is not simply piecemeal or a blended experience. It is a coming together of worship traditions with a purpose and understanding of what it is that we are doing. We know the source of our tradition and draw from it. *ReConnecting Worship* remembers the family of origin and connects us to the "why," the "for whom," and the "what for."

What will application of the principal of ReConnecting mean for us as we plan and develop worship and as we understand worship forms that are different from our own? It is to this question that we will turn our attention in the next section of this resource.

Chapter Four Connections

Prayer

Pray for someone you know who does not have a church home. Ask God to help you see what makes up their world.

Presence

During the week, seek out a restaurant or store you have never experienced. If you have a favorite coffee shop, find a different one for a day. If you shop at the same grocery store, find one unfamiliar to you and buy your groceries there this week. Seek out a restaurant with a different type of food from which you are accustomed to and take your family or yourself there for dinner. At some point during the week, seek out an experience that will be unfamiliar to you.

Planting

This week's connections are particularly relevant to the starting of new congregations. Sensitivity to the visitor is of crucial importance. As you participate in these exercises, imagine yourself as a person who might be visiting your new congregation two years from now.

When you return to the group next week, bring a token of remembrance from your experience, whether positive or negative. In your journal answer the following questions about your experience and be ready to describe your experience to the group.

1. Did you have any anxiety about entering into a new experience?
2. Did you feel welcomed by those you encountered in your experience?
3. Were there people to help guide you or answer questions during your experience?
4. Did you find the newness of the experience exciting or challenging?
5. Would you be open to adding this new experience into your routine of life or did you discover it wasn't for you?
6. If you found yourself out of place in the experience, what might you have done or others have done to make you feel more comfortable?

If you found yourself at home in the experience, what stood out as the key to your feeling of inclusion?

Gifts

If the church is to convey an attitude of hospitality, it is the respon-sibility of all the members of the congregation to participate in this hospitable atmosphere. This responsibility does not fall only to the usher, the greeter, or the pastor. Identify two ways you can participate in this hospitable atmosphere in the life of your worship community.

Service

In some small way, make a connection with the person for whom you have been praying for this week who does not have a church home. How might you initiate a simple conversation with them about something that he or she consider meaningful? This is not a conver-sation or an act to "change" this person; it is an opportunity to take a small step in forming a relationship with someone currently discon-nected from a faith community.

You may find that the connection does allow you to invite them to your worship service.

If you do not feel comfortable inviting someone to your service, identify why you feel this way.

'e' ventures

Reflect on the following questions during 'e' ventures this week:

1. What can the worship community learn from the way the follow-ing sites are providing connection beyond the product?
2. How might online opportunities or resources available on a church website allow people to connect to the weekly worship experience on a deeper level?

Companies today are incorporating innovation and change to con-tinue building relationships with consumers. Have you ever contem-plated what information is provided on the Internet about your favorite candy bar? Check out www.hersheys.com and find informa-tion including available products, stockholder information, and the company commitment to responsibly growing cocoa. You will also find a place just for kids!

The Internet presence of major television networks has been effec-tively established. www.cbs.com, www.abc.com, and www.nbc.com provide show guides, actor information, and opportunities for you to give your opinion about the characters in your favorite drama, sitcom, or reality show. Some reality type television allows you, the viewer, to participate in decisions made on the show through online voting. At www.lifetimetv.com you can play an online game using your personal designer style as well as check out the upcoming week on the television series "Merge." This game models the show format in which the furniture of newlyweds is merged in order to provide a home that accommodates each individual's decorating taste. Check it out by clicking on the Merge link on the website's front page.

Session Four Video

The video segment on the DVD or VHS in the *ReConnecting Worship Kit* that corresponds to this chapter is Session Four: *Change Happens! Do We React Or Do We Respond?*

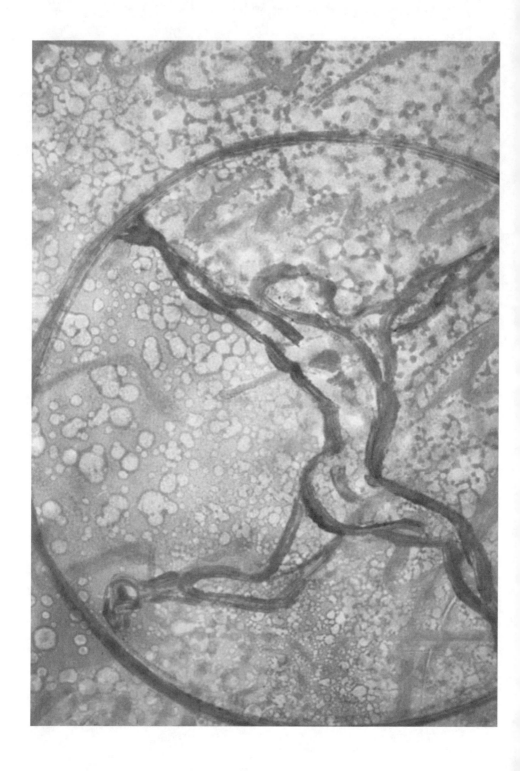

Chapter Five
Worship as the Work
of the
People of God

It was springtime in Louisiana. The ground was wet from the recent and frequent rain. The congregation had gathered for worship as they did each weekend. They sang songs, prayed, and shared their gifts with God through their offerings. As I came forward to preach, some of the members noticed something unusual. Some glanced politely, and some pointed and giggled. It was not usual to see the pastor preparing to preach in muddy rubber boots.

I opened the Bible and read a passage from First Corinthians about the church having many members, but being one body. In the chancel area, next to the communion table, sat a mature woman with a Native American family. She was quilting. As she worked carefully and skillfully on the quilt, I shared that the Scripture reminds us of the way God is like this quilting woman. "God takes the fabric pieces of our individual lives (some worn and faded, some silk, some denim, some cotton print, some exotic) and carefully, stitch-by-stitch, sews them together into one unit, a larger reality than any one individual piece can see or imagine. And when it is finished, the quilt does not exist for itself, but rather to wrap around someone who is cold, to cover a sleeping child, or to give warmth to someone who otherwise would not have cover during the cold night."

I then informed the congregation that I would not be preaching the sermon on that particular day. Instead, the congregation would preach. There was a little nervous movement in the congregation as the people wondered what I had in mind, and if I was going to call on someone to speak. The associate pastor rose and led the congregation in prayer and invited them all, in silence, to rise and walk outside. They rose and processed, in silence, outside where they found a plow with four long ropes attached, stretched out across the wet green grass. A child stood and prayed from a trailer attached to a red pick-up truck. We encouraged all the members of the congregation to take hold of the ropes. "One, two, three, pull!" cried the pastors. And pull they did! The old plow sank deep into the soil and tore through the grass leaving a deep furrow in the otherwise neatly mowed lawn. "Whoa!" shouted the pastors. The congregation stopped pulling and started to cheer. They were preaching the sermon. Together, as one body, they had broken the ground for a new facility that would house the growing number of children and youth who were already part of the congregation, as well as those who were on their way. The sermon had been preached. They had shared in a tangible act of worship as a shared experience and effort. They worshiped in a way that demonstrated the reality of worship as an activity of the Body of Christ.

Marcia McFee explains that "Liturgy" means "the work of the people." This word has, unfortunately, taken on a diminished meaning and is sometimes even considered a "bad word" for those who are attempting to revitalize worship. However, we must reclaim it as key to that very revitalization. More "liturgical" worship will use the voices and words and testimonies and artistic contributions of the people gathered. More "liturgical" worship is not done *to* or *for* the people but *by* the people *for* God."[14]

What does it mean for worship to be the work of the people of God? The word *liturgia* literally means "service." In many cases, the term *liturgy* has come to be understood as the part of the worship service that the congregation reads. Written liturgies can be very effective, but there is a deeper understanding of what liturgy means that can guide us in the creation of faithful, authentic, and meaningful worship services.

Consider what these images of work might have to say to us as we consider the nature of our worship.

Workin' on the chain gang

At the beginning of the movie, *O Brother, Where Art Thou?* a chain gang working out in a field. They are in a line bound by chains, guarded by shotgun-toting officers, and as they sing a song about a man named Lazarus, they swing their hammers in unison and smash rocks. Without dwelling upon what has brought them to the situation of incarceration, imagine for a moment the nature of that work. Swinging hammers, breaking rocks, toiling without purpose—they are "doing time." Work without a purpose is unfulfilling. It is drudgery. Their work was a punishment that had to be endured, and in order to make it through, they had to focus on the fact that if they just kept going, they would get through another day. Some of them, rather than endure the endless purposeless work, chose to escape.

Have you ever been part of a worship service that made you think, "How much longer do I have to sit through this?" or "I wish my pager would go off so I could escape." Sometimes this says more about the attitude of the worshiper than it does about the quality or the content of the worship service, but at other times the experience itself seems to have no purpose or direction and is simply something to be endured. I have spoken to people who see worship as a task to accomplish, a responsibility to be fulfilled, or time to be served. I am reluctant to admit it, but I have found myself in that situation before.

Fast times in the chocolate factory

Remember the *I Love Lucy* television show in which Lucy and Ethel have taken a job in a candy factory and are placed on a chocolate assembly line? As they begin to work, the pace seems calm, but as the scene continues, the speed of the conveyor belt increases so they have to work faster and faster in order to keep up. By the end of the scene the conveyor is moving so fast that chocolates are flying off the end of the conveyor belt and they are stuffing the chocolates in their clothes and in their mouths to hide the fact that they can't keep up.

Life is fast moving, and there are times in the life of a congregation that the pace of activity is so frantic that worship planning and design become much like the experience of Lucy and Ethel—cramming something here or there to hide the fact that we don't have, or haven't taken the time to create, an experience worthy of its purpose. Sadly, I have been there too.

My slot on the assembly line

Henry Ford introduced the assembly line as a process for automobile construction. This method of construction enabled the auto industry to produce a vast number of cars in a short period of time. This method allowed the industry to keep up with the rapidly growing demand for automobiles. As time passed, however, the quality of automobile production decreased as workers became disinterested in the work. Because they worked on only one piece of the automobile, tightening the same bolts of an endless line of automobiles as they passed by, they lost sight of the purpose of their work. They were simply filling slots. They felt disconnected from the larger picture. The work seemed insignificant. Without purpose and a sense of the larger picture, a sense of ownership, pride, and investment was lost. The result was that the quality of work experience and the product declined.

Slot-filling is a practice that, in many ways, has infiltrated the entire structure of the church. Sometimes worship design becomes a process of filling slots. Busy pastors and worship leaders slap together an order of worship as if it were a simple menu-driven process. "We need a call to worship and an opening hymn, then a litany of some sort. What did we use last year on this Sunday? Then a prayer, the children's sermon, the Scripture, some special music, the sermon, the offering, the doxology, and a closing hymn . . . There, we're finished." Worship that is designed as slot-filling or sorting lacks creativity and the power to engage the congregation in the reality of the transforming work of the Body of Christ.

The chain gang was involved in purposeless work. Lucy and Ethel were frantic and reactive. The assembly line workers lost sight of the bigger picture. These images of purposeless, frantic, and slot-filling assembly line work are in many cases very descriptive of the experience of many worship designers as well as worshipers. This type of worship neither nourishes nor shapes healthy Christian community. Worship planners constantly ask, "How can I keep worship fresh?"

A different approach

Perhaps another image of work can give us some insight into a more hopeful model of worship as the work of the people. In the 1980s a man named Lee Iacocca took over as CEO of Chrysler. Sales were sagging. The quality of the automobiles being produced gave a bad name to the words "Made in America." The workforce was in a state of malaise. Iacocca entered this situation and introduced a new methodology for autoworkers. Workers were assigned to teams and given the responsibility for developing the best way to accomplish a particular task to enable the creation of a high-quality car. Each worker was invested in the process and expected to understand the jobs of other people on his or her team, so that if one of the workers (team members) was ill or on vacation, the process could continue. This new process inspired ownership and pride, and fostered commitment and integrity in the industry. This innovative approach took some work, training and time, but the resulting improvement in the quality of the automobiles saved the company from decline. As I have moved through several years of planning and implementing congregational worship experiences, I have discovered that the Iacocca methodology can be applied to worship with powerful results.

In these four images of work, we can see the importance of *purpose, patience,* and *process.* Meaningful worship development requires time. It is a process rather than a task. It is not the work of an individual. It is the work of a congregation that owns the activity, rather than simply observing the performance. It is something that becomes purposeful as the Spirit and the Word of God shape it. If we approach our work with a grasp of these three elements firmly in mind, we can experience a rebirth of energy, creativity, and effectiveness that will inspire, shape, and fill congregations with passionate joy and a strong desire to participate fully in the act of worship.

The service—liturgia—of worship

Rick Warren begins *The Purpose-Driven Life,* with a powerful reminder of the nature of Christian life and work: "It's not about you." Those words apply to the purpose of liturgy as the work of the people of God. If it isn't about me, then what is it about?

The following scriptural texts guide our preparation and implementation of faithful and creative worship. Worship planners can use these five Scriptures as themes to help them ask the right questions about the worship service and the community and thus engage the congregation as participants in worship. The themes are service, love, remember/proclaim, go, and live. Each one is an important facet in worship as the work of the people of God.

Service

So if I, your Lord and Teacher, have washed your feet, you also ought to wash one another's feet. For I have set you an example, that you also should do as I have done to you. (John 13:14-15)

Jesus wanted to insure that the disciples understood that they were not the chosen elite ones who were to be served. They were ones who were to engage in the act of ministry as service, and foot-washing serves to shape the character of Christian discipleship and community. If it were up to me, foot-washing would be considered a sacrament because it is a symbolic act given by Jesus that serves to shape the character of Christian discipleship and Christian community. We have to change the mindset of people who see *worship as something to attend.* Worship is rather an activity of the whole body. It is a shared activity of service. It is not so much that we *attend* the service of worship—as if a worship service was a thing—rather, we *attend to* the service of worship. It is an activity in which all of the members serve God and God's purposes. For worship planners, this means helping the congregation understand that they each have an active role to play in worship and in congregational life.

How can we help people see themselves as active servants of one another during worship? How do we encourage people to understand the importance of their role in making worship meaningful by welcoming newcomers, even as we make an effort to learn and apply the experience to themselves and their lives?

Love

He answered, "You shall love the Lord your God with all your heart, and with all your soul, and with all your strength, and with all your mind; and your neighbor as yourself." (Luke 10:27)

This text seems both clear and familiar. Most Christians recognize it and are able to offer some interpretation of it. Jesus reminds us that the greatest commandment is the commandment to actively love God with all our being and that we are to love neighbor as self. In worship, the body is to use all of its gifts to actively love God and neighbor. For the worship planner, the Scripture evokes the important question of "how?" How do we design worship experiences that call forth response to this greatest commandment? Where and in what ways do we offer opportunities for people to enact these practices in worship?

Remember that people engage the life of faith in different ways. Some people connect to God through emotion, some through understanding, some through contemplation and meditation, and some through using their hands to be creative, or through engaging in mission work. Worship that is truly the work of the people must have handles that each of these types can grasp. Consider your current worship pattern, style, and content. How do they call forth a response of loving activity in the different areas denoted in the commandment to which Jesus referred.

- Heart: Engage the heart and the emotion.
  The issue here is not emotional manipulation but sensitivity to the reality of the heart.
- Mind: Don't check your brain at the door.
  Worship that doesn't affirm those who have questions and challenge the congregation to think about the implications of faith and life fails to engage a major part of what it means to be a human being created in the image of God.

- Soul: Offer opportunities for meditation and reflection.
  Make sure there is space for silence and reflection. Every moment of the service doesn't need to be filled with something. Worship may be one of the only times that some people are able to be still and listen to God.
- Strength: Encourage the engagement of Spiritual gifts.
  How can you offer opportunities for creativity and action?
- Neighbor: Build community, allow for and encourage interaction and point people toward others.

Stories are a powerful way to engage all these areas of the worshiping community. They also can serve to affirm and validate those in the congregation who lead from different facets of faith. Lifting up stories of people who are in service to the community or who use their gifts and creativity to build up the Body of Christ creates a space in the larger story in which such people can see themselves in the picture. It also demonstrates a way to connect for others who have not found places in the community.

In a worship service, we celebrated the return of one of our teams from a medical and construction mission in Mexico. In order to celebrate their accomplishments, affirm and appreciate their contribution, and provide a positive example that others in the congregation might like to follow, we created a video interview of several of the members of the team. It was a simple video of a conversation with four of the participants of various ages, some of whom had been on a mission trip before, and some who went for the first time. They answered questions about the experiences they had, what kind of work they did, if they felt they made a difference, if they had a good time, what kind of effect it had upon them, if they would recommend the experience to others, and if they wanted to go again sometime. In several places the interview footage was overlaid with pictures taken by members of the team while they were in Mexico. This simple video helped the congregation see the work of these individuals as an extension of the ministry of the congregation, gave those who relate to God through service and action something to hold on to, allowed others to experience the mission vicariously through the discussion of the participants, and opened the doors for an invitation to others to consider participating in the next trip.

If a congregation doesn't have access to video editing equipment, the same purpose could be achieved by interviewing some of the participants or showing slides of the mission with brief commentary. Video is desirable because the editor can manage the amount of time that is allotted for sharing the story.

Worship is an act of loving God with our whole being and it calls for us to consider how we engage all the dimensions of this greatest commandment.

Remember/Proclaim

For as often as you eat this bread and drink the cup, you proclaim the Lord's death until he comes. (1 Corinthians 11:26)

Here, in the context of describing the sacrament of communion, Paul teaches the congregation at Corinth that they are not passive recipients of the grace of God in Christ. They are people who actively participate in *remembering* the sacrifice of Christ, and in their very participation become *agents of proclamation.* The sacraments are the center of the worship life of the congregation. Too often it seems that celebrations of the sacraments are tacked on to worship as tasks to be accomplished rather than as powerful, tangible, and symbolic acts that contain the heart of theology. The sacraments are also designed to make worship a real work of the people. The activity of worship through the sacrament makes each participant a preacher, a teller of the story, and a living representative of the gift that Jesus has given and that is still being shared with a broken and hurting world. In communion and in baptism, the community of faith participates in the ongoing work of God's grace and ministry of perpetual reconciliation. The acts of remembrance and proclamation become the work of the people—the work of the body of Christ.

In the video segment, you hear the story of my son and his experience at the worship retreat. His experience of the reality of the sacred message led him to realize that he was not simply a person who lives in the story of God but that he was also person who has the blessing and the responsibility of sharing that story with others. We examined what had taken place in his experience and tried to discern what in that situation might be replicable. The five principles named were 1) With people, 2) Learned the story, 3) Shared in telling the story, 4) Hospitable communication and 5) Entered shared sacred space. Take a moment to consider ways in which your worship experiences provide opportunities for participants to live out these principles.

1) How do or could we provide multigenerational interaction?
   - Encourage fellowship and conversation
   - Allow time for people to greet one another
   - Allow the children to ask questions and respond to them honestly in the context of worship

What other ways might develop this facet of worship?

_____

_____

_____

2) How do or could we learn the story?
   - Instead of reading the Scripture, can the story be retold?
   - Is the Scripture story set in context?
   - Could Sunday school classes study the same Scripture that is used in worship?

   _____

   _____

   _____

3) How do or could we offer opportunities and encourage participants to share in telling the story?
   - Children share artwork as part of the worship service
   - Children and youth participate with the adults in providing music or drama
   - Who in the congregation might be able to contribute as liturgist, reader, storyteller, dancer, musician, greeter?

   _____

   _____

   _____

4) How do or could we structure our worship experiences in word, music, liturgy, etc. to engage people in hospitable communication?
   - Print in the bulletin or project prayers that are memorized by most of the congregation for those who aren't familiar with them
   - Don't assume "insider knowledge" of the church or the Scriptures (this doesn't mean "dumbing down" the content of the service—simply make the content accessible to guests)
   - Communicate in a variety of media forms—props, examples, stories, video, projected images, artwork

   _____

   _____

   _____

5) How do or could we recognize and celebrate shared sacred space?

Have you ever been in a worship service where the Spirit of God was moving in the life of the community through music, or message, or testimony, or interaction and had someone stop the service and reflect on what was happening? "Do you see what is going on here? Do you see the way that God is bringing us together and shaping us into a community of faithful followers? I am overwhelmed by the privilege of sharing in this activity to which God has led us—an activity that recognizes the presence of the Creator and allows us to be part of that ongoing work of creation. Do you see the way God is touching these children and, through that touch, giving us a hope for the future?" Sometimes just stepping outside the normal flow of worship and naming what is happening can give participants a deeper perspective on the sacred nature of what they are experiencing.

_____

_____

_____

Go

Go therefore and make disciples of all nations, baptizing them in the name of the Father and of the Son and of the Holy Spirit, and teaching them to obey everything that I have commanded you. And remember, I am with you always, to the end of the age. (Matthew 28:19-20)

These words of Jesus remind us that the response of the worshiping community is not simply an internal response. Our relationship with Christ points us outward. One image that has been helpful to me as I consider this Scripture and how it relates to the act of worship is that of a pebble in the water. When a person enters Christian community through baptism, that experience is not limited to the life of the individual or to the activity of the community of faith of which they become a part. As a pebble dropped into water causes ripples expaninding outward in motion, so too are the lives of the baptized to have an ever-expanding effect on the surrounding world.

Cathy Townley reminds us that people beyond the walls of the church are also the ones who are to contribute to the shaping of our worship services. "The largest segment of the worship design team is those who aren't yet part of worship, be they unchurched or dechurched. In any church, there are always more who aren't there than are there."[15]

Have you ever considered those who are not even part of your church as part of the worship design team? Have you ever considered that those who are yet to come have already been given gifts that could become part of the congregation's worship?

- How do we as worship designers help to encourage, support, and celebrate that inverted movement?
- How do we remind ourselves of the needs, the language, and the worldviews of those beyond the church with whom we are called to be in ministry?
- How do we remind worshipers that their worship in action and attitude is a witness of the nature and depth of their faith to those who have or may come to peer in to worship?
- How are members of the congregation empowered to share in the evangelistic activity of the gospel?

These questions are critical to the understanding of worship as the work of the people and worship as the activity of the Body of Christ.

Live

I appeal to you therefore, brothers and sisters, by the mercies of God, to present your bodies as a living sacrifice, holy and acceptable to God, which is your spiritual worship. (Romans 12:1)

In this passage, Paul encourages the Christians in Rome to live out lives transformed by the power of God in the world. They have been given the gift of salvation, and part of the response expected of them is to live as renewed and transformed individuals, no longer shaped by the old ways, but by God to think and act in new ways. Worship planners must ask the following: How is our worship experience, designed to encourage transformed lives, building a transformed world? In what ways are the experiences of worship and the call to transformation made tangible and transferable?

- Some churches provide daily Scripture readings in the bulletins to help reinforce the message during the week.
- Some churches provide practical application suggestions for putting the message to work in the world.

- Some churches provide activities to be shared with families or friends during the week that raise deeper questions about the application of the theme or message of the worship service.
- One church provided each worship participant with a sticky note printed with the phrase "It's not about me," to place on the dashboard, the refrigerator door, or in a school notebook.

Can you think of other ways to make the experience of worship tangible and transferable?

_____

_____

_____

These five Scriptures lead us to understanding our purpose as service, love, remember/proclaim, go, and live. These Scriptures and the questions they raise can help those given the task of designing worship direction for imagining ways to create worship experiences that evoke participatory, transformational, and contagious response. Of course these are not the only Scriptures that shape the nature of our worship life together. When we learn to use the Scriptures as lenses through which we interpret the shape of our worship life, we will be provided with an endless source of challenge and inspiration.

Spontaneous liturgy[16]

During the broadcasts about the terrorist attacks on September 11, 2001, one image in particular rises to the forefront of my consciousness a week later as I stare at the pile of papers on my desk. A blizzard of paper swirled and drifted like snow, flooding the streets, telling the stories of activities which had suddenly and unexpectedly ceased. The piles of papers on my desk seem somewhat less significant. In my lap, however, is a big pile of paper that tells a different story. This pile of paper tells the stories of children and prayer. These papers contain a link to God and the heart of children and are destined for the same streets already overburdened with paper. They are not *stories about children and prayer*; they are *the prayers of children*. I should step back a few days and explain the story of their origin.

Tuesday night, after the attack, we gathered the leadership of the church together to pray, to share, to determine needs both within and beyond the congregation, and to strategize our response. People spoke of anger, fear, confusion, worry about how children would be affected by the crisis, and mostly the feeling of helplessness. It was not a helplessness that comes from lack of resource or ability but a helplessness that comes from lacking a clear target of need. If it had been a famine, we would have gathered food. If it had been a hurricane, we could have gone to work and physically aided in the cleanup. People want a tangible way to respond to suffering.

In this case, other than giving blood, donating money, and offering prayers, there was not anything that we could do immediately to respond—we were already doing those things. Furthermore, there were wounds in the church family to be bound up, tears to be shared, and questions to be addressed. We needed to build community, provide comfort, encouragement, and direction, focus on God, lift prayers, and reach out to the community at Ground Zero. And, we needed to begin the process by *this weekend*. Tangible. Prayers needed to become tangible.

The next morning, one of our Stephen Ministers, who is also a small-group leader and a woodworker, suggested that he and his small group could make a bunch of simple crosses for people to hold as they prayed. That's good, I thought; that is tangible. It would also give him something to focus on and allow his group to come together with a purpose. Yes . . . tangible . . . we weren't there yet, but it was a start.

Next, we thought of a wailing wall. I had seen it before. People go there to mourn and pray and weep, and many times place written prayers in the spaces between the stones. The paper in the cracks doesn't help the prayers get to the ears of God, but it does something for the person who prays. It is tangible. Butcher paper on the walls and colored markers became our wailing walls. Yet I knew that if everyone were to try to get up and get to the wall there would not be enough room or time. Some wouldn't want to get up, and also, while it would be helpful for the one writing the prayer, how would that become tangible to the people at Ground Zero? Tangible and transferable . . .

We decided that we would provide every worshiper with a piece of paper, a pen, a piece of yarn, and one of the wooden crosses that were being made so that everyone could participate in writing a prayer for someone who was suffering as a result of the tragic attack. We also wanted to make sure that the children were included. It needed to be a time of togetherness. We needed that. We wanted them to be close and to be able to allow them to feel safe and at home in the church. It was family time, not a time to send the children elsewhere so we could talk about the "real issues."

The preparations required a willingness to change plans, flexibility, and a little extra running around, but by the weekend we were ready. Paper had been cut and inserted in the bulletins. Baskets had been prepared holding crosses, yarn, and pens. Big baskets filled with stacks of paper and boxes of crayons became receptacles of expression for the children (and for some parents and the pastors). I asked all the children to come forward and to gather around close. As they came, I invited the adults to pay attention, and to overhear what was going on with the children, because we would all be participating in a project together and I needed their help.

First I asked questions—what had they seen? What did they understand about what was happening? "A plane hit a big building and a lot of people died." "People are trying to break up our country." "Firemen died trying to help rescue the people." "Some people helped keep the fourth plane from killing more people in Washington."

Then I asked about feelings. Some of them were hesitant to share, but slowly they opened up. "I feel sad for the people who died." "I'm scared." "It makes me really mad that people would do this." "I wish I could help them, but I don't know how."

The honest voices of the children expressed innocently the feelings that everyone in the congregation was feeling. After trying to reassure them that God was with us and with the ones who were hurting, and reminding them that there were lots of people in America and all around the world working hard to keep them safe, we began to turn the corner to response.

"Now, I need your help. Imagine being there in New York or Washington, and you are a fireman or other rescue worker and you have been working really hard. Maybe you know someone who was in the building that collapsed. Maybe you are in a hospital, because you were injured. Imagine how they are feeling. I know we all want to do something to help, and many are giving blood and we are collecting money to send through the Red Cross and the United Methodist Committee on Relief, but they also need prayer. This morning, let's pray for all of those who are struggling and suffering right now, and do it in a way that it won't be just us and God who know that we are praying. Someone out there, someone whose name we don't even know, will know we are praying as well." As we were handing out the paper and the crayons to the children and they were spreading out on the floor to create their colorful, tangible prayers, the baskets of pens, yarn, and crosses were passed out through the rest of the congregation. To help people get started, I had a written a few suggested ideas which were being projected on the screen. The flutist started to play as the people began to pray and write. What happened was *spontaneous liturgy*.

The work of the people poured forth in hearts with great passion and intention. The colors and the words flowed from the fingers of the little ones sitting and lying down on the carpeted floor in front of the altar. The walls filled with creative expression. One man attending the service, a Jew, wrote in Hebrew, the Hebrew mourner's prayer. Our intern pastor from Tonga wrote a prayer in Tongan. Never have I seen so many people so focused and so intense. Even the children colored and wrote with intensity and compassion. As some finished and some continued, a couple of people began to walk some of the pictures around the worship area showing them silently to the gathered family. The innocent compassion and simplicity of the crayon prayers brought tears to the eyes of many.

Then we prayed corporately. All of the children piled up their prayers and we placed our hands on them. The adults in the seats held their crosses, rolled scrolls of tangible transferable prayer, and we all lifted up our prayers to God. As we received the offering, people were invited to place their prayers in the baskets along with their financial contributions. The children's prayers were spread out and displayed on the altar. Some of the children didn't want to stop. They wanted to create more prayers, so we let them continue to color in the baptismal area while I preached. They were quiet, focused, and intent on continuing the spontaneous liturgy of crayons and compassion.

Many things happened that morning, not all of them planned. Children saw adults cry and comfort one another. They saw it happening in church and they saw them pray. They prayed with them in their own words and images. We sang together with deep emotion and compassion. These were rich moments of human wholeness and authenticity in a sometimes emotionally sterile environment. These were moments wherein the crushing reality of the terrorist attack, which for many seemed surreal in its media distance, entered the gathering of the community, and we saw pieces of each other that we had not seen before.

So, that is how these papers came to be in my lap this morning: the tangible and transferable expression of the prayers of children, destined to reach the ones for whom they prayed. Perhaps, when these pieces of paper reach the streets of New York and Washington, D.C., papers that were indirectly created by the attack, those who see them will not see the senseless, violent end of so many lives, but instead experience the touch of God and the hope of the beginning of a new creation.

Go back over the description of this worship service and try to identify worship as the work of the people. Look particularly for ways in which the service was designed as to encourage the facets and principles explored in this chapter. Make notes in the space provided below. You will have an opportunity to share your reflections as part of the group discussion in the next session.

Serve

_____

_____

Love

_____

_____

Remember/Proclaim

_____

_____

Go

_____

_____

Live

_____

_____

In case you are wondering, the papers did reach New York. The childrens' prayers were delivered to a command post where rescue workers, doctors, and nurses would come to rest between shifts. We received a letter about the effect they had as, one by one, tired workers would come back to the command center to rest on one of the many cots that filled the room. As they entered the room, many of the workers would take a prayer and a cross, or a child's crayon prayer drawing and read it while they lay on the cots. Many of them took the prayers and drawings with them as they went back to Ground Zero and passed them on to others. I shared with the congregation the letter telling of the outcome of their tangible, transferable prayers. They were encouraged to know that the ripples of their worship were being felt and that they were part of God's larger working in the world.

We opened this chapter with the image of the congregation using the plow to break the ground so that the project would be the work of the people. The pastor's task was not to push the plow, or even to break the ground. The pastor's task was to call the people together, to encourage them to participate, to keep the plow pointed in the right direction, and to make sure it stayed in the ground. The plow, powered by the people, like a quilting needle in the hand of God, touched the earth and stitched the continuation of the kingdom. Such is the nature of worship as the work of the people.

The next three chapters offer suggestions and perspectives to enable your congregation to begin to move in this direction. It is not a movement to one particular style or another, but rather a process and a methodology that can improve the worship of any congregation and any style of worship. In chapter six, Stacy explores the process of locating and developing resources for worship as well as discovering and calling forth the gifts of the congregation. In chapter seven, she unpacks the process and nature of developing and implementing faithful and innovative worship with a creative ministry team. In the final chapter, I provide a worship planning process and a method for planning worship a year at a time that may serve as an image to help guide your congregation in worship planning. This process encourages prayerful preparation and faithful use of Scripture, tradition, reason and experience to engage the diverse gifts, languages and needs of your congregation.

Chapter Five Connections

Prayer

Pray for people in your congregation who plan worship each week. You may be one of those people! Pray that the resources and elements might come forth to provide an authentic and engaging worship experience.

Presence

Take a walk. Be aware of the way the different parts of your body work together as you walk. Notice how your eyes, ears, heart, lungs, feet, and the rest of your body all interact to move you along. Imagine the different gifts of the congregation working together as one body to walk the "walk" of worship.

Planting

Visit a church in your community and carefully observe what systems are present or missing to welcome and care for you as a visitor. How will you shape your new congregation's hospitality system?

Gifts

Your church offers visitors a gift each week—a gift of worship. As you attend your weekly worship service, attend "as a visitor." Experience this gift from the perspective of someone attending your facility and your service for the first time. Approach the entire experience as a person who has never attended. From the time you enter the parking lot, do so with "visiting eyes." Where should you park? Where is the worship area? Do you need a nursery? Would you like some coffee? When you participate in the worship service be aware of the things you might not know as a visitor. For instance, the Lord's Prayer, the Doxology, or the Great Thanksgiving may be foreign to you; baptism or communion might make you uncomfortable if you do not understand the meaning. In your journal, list those pieces of your worship experience that were foreign to you as well as affirming to you as a "visitor." When you return to the group next week you will have an opportunity to share your experience.

Service

How do you love God with your heart, mind, soul, strength, and neighbor as self through the worship experience? Refer to page 97 as a guide to process your response. Remember, each person will respond to the question in a different way.

Heart:

_____

_____

Mind:

_____

_____

Soul:

_____

_____

Strength:

_____

_____

Neighbor:

_____

_____

'e' ventures

As you reflect on the Body of Christ working together this week, visit www.medtropolis.com and click on the "Visit the Virtual Body" link. Try your hand at building a skeleton or organizing your organs! Notice the effective way in which the site's interactive and visual nature provides a better understanding as to the inner workings of the human body. How might the church more effectively demonstrate the Body of Christ working together in the world? Be prepared: this is not a deep theological experience. Have fun!

Session Five Video

The video segment on the DVD or VHS in the *ReConnecting Worship Kit* that corresponds to this chapter is Session Five: *One Generation Shall Tell Another.*

Chapter Six
Infusing Imagination

On a beautiful, shady afternoon, children quickly removed their socks and shoes and found a place on the edge of the canvas stretched out across the asphalt parking lot. The canvas was a large burlap drop cloth from the local hardware store. Adults held pans containing washable paint. The adults walked around the large square of seated children and, as the children stuck their feet in the air, the adults brushed the bottoms of their feet with paint. Then the children carefully and thoughtfully walked back and forth upon the canvas, reflecting on what it might have been like to walk alongside Jesus during the last week of his life.

This painting project took place the week before Palm Sunday. The children were creating the altar cloth for the worship service. Before the painting began the leader read the Scripture of Jesus entering Jerusalem on a donkey. The group discussed what that last week must have been like for Jesus. They talked about how the disciples must have felt—first excitement and then fear. As they worked together to create the huge cloth that would be used in the service entitled, "Walking Today, Where Jesus Walked," they were encouraged to think not only about walking alongside Jesus when he was here on earth, but also about what it means to walk with Jesus in the present day. The children were not only participating in the creation of the weekly worship experience, but also growing in their own faith journey.

The idea for this incorporation of the children did not come from a resource book or prepackaged sermon series. The idea came from someone with eyes open to the needs of the congregation and the service; someone aware of seeking out ways to include as many multigenerational connections to the service as possible; someone aware of creativity merging with the spiritual growth and faith journey of the congregation.

Robb Redman, in, *The Great Worship Awakening*, states, "The crisis that faces most churches now is not the lack of resources but rather the failure of imagination to use the resources God has already given."[17] When congregations investigate creative ways to enhance weekly worship, the unknown seems overwhelming. Where does one find all these creative ideas? What book or resource is going to provide the answers?

What course can be taken to provide the knowledge? A sense of inadequacy can set in before an attempt is made to try something new.

The process one uses for resource acquisition and worship planning can help answer these questions. Instead of the focus being placed on "where to find," the focus needs to be placed on "how to find." One image that can help us with the process of acquiring resources is found in the old folk tale "Stone Soup."

Once upon a time, somewhere in Europe, there was a great famine. People hoarded whatever food they could find, hiding it from their friends and neighbors. One day a peddler drove his wagon into a village and began asking questions as if he planned to stay for the night.

"There's not a bite to eat in the whole area," he was told. "Better keep moving on."

"Oh, I have everything I need," he said. "In fact, I was thinking of making some stone soup to share with all of you." He pulled an iron cauldron from his wagon, filled it with water, and built a fire under it. Then, with great ceremony, he drew an ordinary-looking stone from a bag and dropped it into the water.

By now, hearing the rumor of food, most of the villagers had come to the square. As the peddler sniffed the "broth" and licked his lips in anticipation, hunger began to overcome their skepticism.

"Ahh," the peddler said to himself rather loudly, "I do like a good stone soup. Of course, stone soup with *cabbage*—that's hard to beat."

Soon a villager approached hesitantly, holding a cabbage he'd retrieved from its hiding place, and added it to the pot. "Wonderful!" cried the peddler. "You know, I once had stone soup with cabbage and a bit of salt meat as well, and it was fit for a king."

The village butcher managed to find some salt meat . . . and so it went, through potatoes, onions, carrots, mushrooms, and so on, until there was indeed a delicious meal for all.

The villagers offered the peddler a great deal of money for the magic stone, but he refused to sell and traveled on the next day. And from that time on, long after the famine had ended, they reminisced about the finest soup they'd ever had.[18]

The role of those involved in worship design is to call forth the ingredients hidden and held by the members of the congregation and the community. The art of acquiring these resources for worship does not correspond to a particular worship genre. You need appropriate resources whenever designing traditional, contemporary, or other worship situations. If you use an organ or a guitar, an orchestra or a band, a screen or a hymnal, robes or Birkenstocks, you still seek high quality resources. You desire components that will speak the language of those engaging in worship. You build the basics into worship that will convey an attitude of hospitality to those who have not yet experienced the love and grace of Jesus Christ. Your "stone soup" will be superb, but it will be unlike that of any other congregation.

Below you will not find a list of places to purchase the latest, excellent resources required to enhance your current worship setting. You will find a process for the acquisition of resources and a way to plan your work that does not attach to any stylistic category. You will observe a thought process concerning resources and planning for worship that is an attitude and a way of life, an expression of the gifts and stories of God's people. This attitude presumes that *imagination is not exclusive to a particular style of worship.*

Each example or idea might not be one that would work in your particular situation. What works in one congregation's experience may not be effective in another, even within the same stylistic category of worship. However, the process discussed in this chapter *will* have application for your situation. This process is proven in many different worship "styles."

By allowing your imagination to merge with God's creative and redemptive work, you can enhance any worship setting, regardless of the style or size of the worship community.

Focusing on faith

He was small. The giant was big. No one else felt confident in taking on the task of defeating the Philistines. The majority of the Israelites responded to giant Goliath's intimidating challenge with fear. Saul and his army were so focused on the overwhelming nature of the task at hand that a solution to the problem could not been seen. It was David, the small boy, who approached the situation with a different view. He viewed the situation through eyes of faith. It was David's trust in God that allowed him to see the task of defeating Goliath as a possibility.

When church leaders listen in the present day to the call to create and implement worship in new ways, the task often seems as overwhelming as Goliath's "challenge" to the Israelites. "We are too small to step into a new format of worship planning." "We do not have the money or resources to incorporate new experiences into weekly worship." "We do not have the creative people in our congregation that the megachurches have in their congregations." "Worship creation and implementation in a new way sounds too risky. What if it doesn't work?" "What if it interferes with Sunday School?" It is with these thoughts that the fear causes a stalemate. Leaders realize something needs to be done, but day after day things continue as they always have been done, and the challenge from the "giant" continues to be heard. How can the sense of fear and intimidation associated with innovative and creative approaches to worship be transformed into a positive and energized attitude of faith? What can we learn from David's response to Goliath's challenge?

Overcoming doubt and opposition

By stepping into a new way of creating and implementing worship, either in an existing congregation or a new church start, we live out a sense of calling. If God is calling a congregation to do something in a new way, then God is not calling the congregation to do it alone. The call might seem overwhelming at times, but it is with an attitude of faith and trust in God that a sense of peace can be found. Prayer, planning, and vision casting work together to allow God's call to become a reality. The lens through which one chooses to view the call of stepping out into new territory determines the success of its outcome.

Church leaders often feel obligated to overlay a model of worship planning and implementation that is successful in another church setting. When attempting to move forward with new approaches to worship, your own setting will define a different set of effective processes. Studying the experience of other congregations is very important; attempting to copy a particular model will cause only frustration. It is often the attempt to overlay a pre-existing structure of worship planning and implementation that leads to paralysis, feeling weighted down by a sense of failure and shrinking back from the task at hand.

If you take a group of people to Willow Creek, Ginghamsburg, Community Church of Joy, Windsor Village UMC, St. Luke's Community in Dallas, or even my own setting for a church conference, your group will probably be overwhelmed—excited but overwhelmed. Expect to broaden the scope of possibility in your own setting rather than recreate the structure and format you have experienced. Every congregation's first step will look different. It is the leader's task to reframe the knowledge and experiences of others by offering the big picture, placing the changes in worship in the context of church history, particular tradition, and available resources.

Make it a combo, please.

The "make it a combo, please" mentality of our culture often stifles the creative resources within a congregation. We live in a society that sees prepackaged deals as a convenience. Much of what we purchase today lacks originality because "prepackaging" is a popular way to lower cost, and it helps us avoid overshooting the needs of the user or buyer. A travel kit with soap, shampoo, conditioner, toothpaste, and deodorant makes packing much easier. Driving through a fast food chain and ordering my favorite item by number in combo form makes the service even faster. However, approaching new and creative forms of expression in worship through a "prepackaged" lens can hinder the creative energy required to reconnect.

I remember tossing and turning the night before the first day of school. The first day of school landed at the top of life's most exciting moments (alongside Christmas day). Beyond the excitement of finding out the teacher I would have for the year and the friends who would be my classmates, the first day of school meant the school supply list would be available. Which cartoon character would be on the folder carried back and forth to school? Would erasable pens be allowed this year? Will we use colored pencils? Would we be able to use college ruled paper? Most importantly, would we be allowed to have the sixty-four-color box of crayons with the sharpener? The selection of school supplies was the highlight of the back-to-school season. The items that would fill my desk would serve as creative tools for the entire year. Today I watch as many parents write a check and a prepackaged school supply kit is handed to the child on the first day of school. This level of convenience can save parents two or three exhausting trips to the world's biggest superstore, but I'm glad this option was not available when I was a child!

The prepackaged syndrome will probably sustain the "slot filling" practice of worship planning, which was discussed in Chapter Five. The incorporation of items from life is what makes a worship experience dynamic. No *one* book or resource is going to provide everything your congregation needs for worship. Prepackaged resources can be used, but they will simply become stones in your bag, not the whole bag itself. Ideas and resources from a variety of sources need to be incorporated into worship. Many individuals and congregations share creative pieces and ideas to be used in worship. This is excellent.

It is the matching of pieces from all the resources available today, combined with the gifts of those within the congregation, that produces creative worship within a congregation. Original resources from within your own congregation—art, photography, creative movement, music, poetry, drama, pottery, stained glass, digital media—will flourish. Even gifts that might not be seen as worship resources, such as building video platforms, choir risers, or sound cabinets, can be incorporated into worship in many ways when people know the abilities God has given them can be used as a resource. This thought process not only allows for "liturgy" to come from the people, but also saves a huge amount of money, creating a healthy balance.

When attempting to approach new forms of worship, church leaders often find the equipment and resources of other churches overwhelming. Some congregations may be blessed initially with the financial means to buy all the latest "bells and whistles" now seen in larger worshiping congregations, but most churches acquire resources as they grow. A certain amount of financial resources is necessary to create a basic framework for implementation of innovative worship, but this too will vary from church to church. Stepping forward with quality in content and execution is much more important than stepping forward with impressive capital. Viewing worship as a life experience will yield more resources than you can imagine.

Unleashing the creativity of the Body of Christ

It was an hour before worship, and the altar wasn't finished. Mary realized she didn't have enough hydrangeas, but she needed only a few bundles to complete the altar. As she hurried out the door of her shop to solve the problem, she noticed a woman broken down in the parking lot where her car was parked. The woman said, "Could you please help me? I cannot get home." Even though the clock was ticking, Mary told the woman to hop in her car and she would take her home. Mary knew she could not leave the woman stranded. After a glance at the gas gauge, she realized she might not make it to the woman's house and to worship, much less find the flowers she needed. As they began to drive, the woman said, "You may want to drop me off at the end of the street because my neighborhood is not too safe." Mary assured her that she didn't mind taking her to her home, very aware of the dangerous nature of the neighborhood. She felt she was doing the right thing and that God would certainly take care of the rest. As they drove to the woman's front door, the woman asked how she could repay Mary. Trying not to seem too overwhelmed, Mary said, "You don't owe me a thing, but could I cut some of the beautiful hydrangeas growing in your front yard to take to my church tonight?" The woman smiled and gladly sent Mary on her way with enough flowers to complete the altar. Mary may have arrived with a gas tank on empty, but a heart full of the presence of God's ever-surrounding love and care. The altar in worship that evening was beautiful and had touched lives before the service ever began.

The leadership key to unlocking imagination and creativity is teaching people to live with their eyes open to experiencing God in every moment of life. Give the worship team a permission slip to share the ingredients that they posses for the stone soup of the congregation. Painting a picture of this preferred future allows "seeing" to become "being." This type of visionary leadership is one of the primary keys to unlocking the creativity of the Body of Christ.

Margaret J. Wheatly asks this question in *Turning To One Another*: "What am I willing to notice in my world?"[19] It is with this type of focus in daily living that those in worship leadership become more aware of resources that will speak to a variety of people within the congregation and to those yet to experience God outside the walls of the worshiping community. When this heightened awareness is combined with a sense of imagination, resources become usable. To illustrate how ordinary alertness is operative in generating creativity, here are examples of various needs that a worship director or coordinator might pose for any given weekend.

- We need wooden stars that children can paint them each week during Advent to bring them to the manger scene on Christmas Eve. Would you cut those out for us in your woodworking shop?
- We need a background of trees for the drama in worship. Could we borrow some from your nursery for the weekend?
- There is a spoken liturgy for worship next weekend and you would be wonderful for one of the parts. Would you participate?

- Someone told me you have danced in the local dance company since you were a child. Could you participate with our college creative movement team?
- We need a new communion pitcher and set of chalices. Knowing you love to paint pottery, would you paint a new set for worship?

Questions like these incorporate a diverse group of people into the ordinary acts of creation each week. Imagination may be the only valuable resource you are missing, and you really cannot pay enough to buy it. It is already present in the work of the people. Harry Connick, Jr.'s song entitled *There Is Always One More Time* has a line in it that states, "Keeping your eyes closed is worse than being blind." When people begin to view life with open eyes to see each and every moment as an expression of God's activity in the world, creativity flows.

Standards for selection of worship resources

From Chapter Two we remember that, "Every ritual and litany, every song or drama, every sermon or sacrament exists to orient God's people towards God and to build communal life around that shared orientation." Each act of worship connects us to God's "why."

Even though we have highlighted the risk of buying prepackaged worship content, which can stifle imagination before it is ever tapped, a growing number of Christian publishing houses and distributors, as well as secular producers of imagery, are emerging. These reference works can be adapted in computer graphics programs by many church office workers, not to mention teenagers and retired computer hobbyists. Image editing is spreading throughout our culture as rapidly as word processing did in the 1990s. Amazing resources are regularly springing forth from within existing congregations.

How does one draw from all of these emerging sources to create a collection of resources that are usable in the local congregation? One suggestion is to let Scripture, Tradition, Experience, and Reason guide the acquisition of resources for the reference shelf, the hard drive, or the worship supply and craft room.

Scripture is at the heart of every worship experience. Any theme or metaphor you choose will be based in Scripture.

The memory of our *tradition* and heritage is necessary in worship planning. New ways to share our past with future generations are part of what it means to exercise the imagination.

How the element will enhance the *experience* of worship, as well as connect with relevance to the experiences of individuals, is a critical indicator of the value of the worship component. The impact of a worship element is directly linked to inclusiveness and hospitality in the worship environment.

Reason enables us to keep the other standards in check as we look to incorporate each element into worship. *The use of creative or innovative elements merely for the sake of use alone, coolness, or applause does not produce authentic worship that is oriented to God.*

The worship leadership team will need training in how to apply these standards until they become so much a part of the planning process that they are not used as a litmus test or as an escape into intellectual analysis that stifles creativity. A better use of the standard is to apply it when navigating and searching for resources that will help fit on the resource shelf or hard drive.

The resource adventure

Where does the search begin in the basic areas of worship creation as leaders set out to create authentic and vibrant worship? The search begins by assessing your current search process. Where do the current resources used for your worship experience come from? What is the current process used in the search for resources? Who contributes to this process? As simplistic or complicated as this answer might be, take a few minutes to evaluate where some of your resources are currently acquired.

Where are the following resources acquired that are used in your current worship service? If you are a new church start or looking to start an alternative service in an established congregation, what has been your previous experience in acquiring resources for the following:

Music:

_____

_____

Litanies:

_____

_____

Prayers:

_____

_____

Images:

_____

_____

Hardware:

_____

_____

Other:

_____

_____

Evaluating your current situation is part of the challenge. You want to build upon the strength of your previous experience. Identifying your current search process may also highlight areas that may not be working effectively.

From the digital world come many helpful tools available for the search. Let's take a look at how the Internet interacts with daily life experiences and current culture to enhance the worship experience.

Music

Nearly everyone has purchased some type of compact disc while not really knowing what type of music it would contain. Most companies now put short music segments on their websites. Many lyric sites as well as individual artist websites contain the lyrics to almost any song you can imagine. You can even go to a website that contains the lyrics to older public domain hymn tunes. You can listen to the hymn tune while you read the lyrics! You may have heard a song on the radio, in a restaurant, at a movie, or at a concert and chances are great that you can find it somewhere on the Internet. You can better evaluate what you experience or what someone might suggest to you before purchasing it for worship. This ability to search through music allows for a larger percentage of music to be researched and a large amount of money to be saved on unusable resources. You can also determine what formats are available for purchase. Is there a choral arrangement of the piece you would like to use? Is there sheet music with chords? Is there an orchestral arrangement? Is there a site that has the song available to download and purchase (e.g., www.jwpepper.com, www.tismusic.com, www.sheetmusicplus.com, www.sheetmusicdirect.com, and Cokesbury.com)? Often you only need to find which format is available on the Internet, and a local store will have the product available. Regardless of whether a piece of music was written in the 1800s or the current year, you will probably be able to find it in its available form on the Internet.

Digital imagery and video

The incorporation of digital images in worship services is growing rapidly. The Internet is full of websites with images for church use. If you type "images for worship" in a search engine, one of the first sites that appears is a church that offers free images for use in other worshiping communities. Some churches and individuals post to sites and grant other churches permission to use the images they have created. Many websites contain reasonably priced discs full of worship images. Commercial sites also target people who work with image-based projects, allowing downloadable images for a fee (i.e. www.digitaljuice.com, www.crystalgraphics.com, www.worshipimages.com). Some publishers are releasing image collections on CD-ROM, such as *Abingdon Worship Photos*, which is one way to build a reference shelf of images that are available when needed.

A growing number of video resources are available. Popular movie clips reinforce the theme of the worship service and also many companies produce videos designed specifically for worship around topical themes. Short dramatic or documentary style videos are popular. Also, image-based videos that set up a particular theme can be found (e.g., worshipconnection.com, www.harbingeronline.com, www.midnightoilproductions.net, and www. highwayvideo.com). Once you find what you are looking for, you can decide whether it can be purchased locally or whether you want to order it via the Internet.

Digital imagery and video can often inspire the creation of your own media. When your congregation realizes you are looking for digital imagery, a whole new set of people will spring to life who might participate in worship. An awareness of the gifts of these individuals allows worship leaders to share upcoming themes so that specific pieces can be created for an upcoming service. What can be done with consumer-grade digital cameras and digital video cameras would have been unbelievable ten years ago. Have you ever watched a twelve-year-old child manipulate still photos or edit video on a basic editing program?

You can never have too many images or video clips from which to choose. You might use a single image one weekend and ten images the next. Then again, a video clip might be used only once a month. The goal is to develop an image and video database from commercial products and original creation. At the beginning this data might be stored on someone's home computer (just as our membership rolls and financial reports were stored on our treasurer's PC ten years ago.) As creativity emerges you will bring these processes into the church office, so you can sort and search through the assets.

The amount of Internet supply is too lengthy to list and constantly evolving. Are you in need of sermon ideas, drama scripts, service outlines, litanies, or poetry? Would you like to compare the prices of the latest projectors, sound equipment, or paraments? The Internet allows a portal to access information and supplies in a way that was previously impossible. One emerging portal is now designed for you: WorshipConnection.com.

These are by no means inclusive of all the valuable websites available to you; it is simply a place to begin for those who may never have done this type of research before.

Ministry resources

Another valuable worship resource comes from the activity of the various ministry areas within your congregation. Because of the visibility of the church gathered, most leaders realize that it is crucial to feature the life of the community beyond the worship service. In *Mission Driven Worship: Helping Your Changing Church Celebrate God,* Handt Hanson writes, "If we simply create worship services that are unrelated to our organic existence as a complete system, that is exactly what our services will continue to be: unrelated."[20] Opportunities such as outreach, teaching, study, and small groups may never connect potential disciples to a ministry unless they experience ministry. Further, unless the disciple is sent forth with a taste of the ministry. Worship itself will not become a way of life. "Ministry moments" allow many opportunities to be made unaware of the life work that is taking place in and through the members of the congregation. Mission moments include sharing the life-changing effects of a mission trip or outreach program, participating in the children's ministry, care ministry, or youth ministry, or sharing the way in which someone has been recipients of the love and care of a ministry area. These experiences are shared through a personal testimony, short video clip, or a written liturgy.

A resource-full life

As worship leadership begins to encourage and allow creative elements to unfold within the worship setting, more opportunities and ideas begin to surface. Thoughts and ideas will come from different people and different places. Having someone to help process the thoughts and ideas of others is helpful. Begin by identifying a couple of people who are interested in contributing to worship through this type of research (which usually requires Internet skills). Thus another type of gift can be to be "lived" into the creation of worship.

Finding someone who enjoys seeking out resources and ideas for worship can greatly enhance the worship planning process. Filling the position of "worship researcher" is not usually thought of when listing typical worship roles such as pianist, liturgist, choir member, or usher. However, training someone in the role of "worship researcher" can add a powerful dynamic.

Think about the typical stereotype we place on one who engages in "research" as a profession, such as a research assistant or librarian. We generally think of this person as someone totally engrossed in a particular field of study, one surrounded by books and computers, and one who, by society's standards, might be considered "nerdy." Someone involved in research is constantly reviewing the past and looking towards the future for the answers to the mysteries they seek to uncover. Someone involved in research is passionate about a particular subject area and each new piece of information is a doorway to new possibilities. It is often a small find that causes great joy for the researcher. "Researching" or "resourcing" for worship can be compared to research done in a profession such as medicine or archaeology. Think about how helpful it would be to have someone who views life through a worship lens, someone who researches life and how life (past, present, and future) can help tell God's story. Someone who looks for the latest worship resources; new music, media, drama, books, art, ideas; someone who explores the many intersecting avenues of life and how these avenues might serve to connect us to the part we are called to play in God's story; someone in tune with traditions and history, who allows the past to merge with the present to shape the future. Whether watching TV, searching the Internet, shopping in the grocery store, reading a book, attending a concert, playing with a child, or taking clothes to the laundry, a "worship researcher" evaluates the entire experience through a worship lens. The worship researcher knows that every idea may not become part of the worship experience, but it may lead to something else that will become part of experiencing God in a new way. The worship researcher knows that past and present experiences shape what is to come in the future. The worship researcher knows that the search never ends but a new adventure always awaits.

As I walked into a hospital today to be with someone during surgery I was reminded of how much I dislike hospitals. Within seconds I thought, "I wonder how many people walk into a church and have this feeling? I wonder what it is that causes people to have such a reaction? I wonder how we can help remove this stigma for people hesitant to enter a worship service?"

I watched as a young woman prepared my fruit smoothie at the new wireless Internet café in town. After having experienced several different beverages over my last few visits, it occurred to me that great effort was placed in the presentation of the beverages being served. Great effort had been taken to make sure the atmosphere was inviting and experiential. Much thought was put into the customer's experience. I thought about how this experience could be applied to enhance the planning, preparation, and presentation of worship.

As I watched a show about home "makeovers," a new approach for the mission team occurred to me: What if we did a makeover for a member of the community in need of home repairs? The whole concept of the makeover program could spark a new sense of passion and accomplishment in an area of great need in our community. The way in which we might effectively incorporate the whole process into the worship experience began to unfold in my mind.

When I take digital pictures, I try to capture images that might effectively work in media presentation software. I see the words on the screen with the image before I take the picture. When I hear a piece of music, I categorically place it in my brain as to what thematic topic it would complement in worship. Being a "resource assistant" for me is exciting and a way of life. The more possibilities I search, the more possibilities I find to involve people so that their unique gifts come to life. The more I search, the better equipped I am to help others bring to life the creativity that lives within them. With the same excitement as someone who researches a cure for a disease or a quest for the location of rare artifacts, I search for effective tools for authentic and engaging worship. The passion is driven by the desire that every person on the earth be touched by the love and grace of Jesus Christ, that every person would find his or her place in God's story, and that he or she might find community and connection. Had I not been encouraged and allowed to participate I would never have developed in such an usual ministry position, or developed such a passion for such an usual role.

Every individual has a unique place in God's kingdom here on earth. Finding a person in your own congregation who might find great joy in worship resourcing can greatly increase the materials in your resource bag. This person can begin to answer the question, "Where do I find _____?"

Find one or two people who are truly passionate about becoming "resource assistants" and who will help build the atmosphere of participation needed for creative worship in a congregation. Someone diligently searching will spin ideas and thoughts with others. It may sound unusual to those who learned how to assemble information in seminary, but now it is one viable way for the people of God to live out the gift that God has given.

Worship as life

With a stack of papers and my lunch, I sat working in a local restaurant. I heard someone call my name and saw a smiling member of the congregation running over to greet me. She had recently participated in a worship experience where her gift of painting was a part of the service. Christina donated the work she created to a sale to benefit the youth ministry. She expressed her appreciation at being included in the service and wanted to take a picture of the work before it was sold. "I studied art in college, and my professor told me I had no gift . . . no ability for art. This work of art is the first thing I have created in over a year." Christina and her husband also work with the children's ministry on Sunday mornings. They are part of the team that encourages children to create visual art as part of their participation in God's story each week. Christina's story comes from a stone soup experience. She heard the call to bring forth her ingredient to the "soup" of the congregation. She had hidden that ingredient behind past failures and judgments. Her act of participation and involvement has reawakened a passion within her, allowing her to participate in telling God's story in a new way. Christina brings her life story to worship and to the Christian community she now calls family. She brings herself and her life as one who is being transformed and actively participating in the transformation of the world.

When worship is seen as a way of life, the resources for worship begin to come forth with incredible depth and richness, unique to each worship experience. Cultivating this type of environment for worship resources does take patience; it will not happen overnight. However, the visionary leadership of those planning and leading worship will allow this type of growth to begin. As this type of environment is created, a system for managing and incorporating the gifts of the gathered community becomes necessary. In the next chapter we will take a look at a team-based process that allows these resources to continue to grow and flourish within the Body of Christ.

Chapter Six Connections

Prayer

Is our worship all that it could be? Ask God what challenges we, as a congregation, are facing in worship. What resources do we need? What is holding us back?

Presence

Using the disposable cameras you received in the last session, answer the following questions:

- Where do you see God loving?
- Where do you see God's people serving?
- Where do you see God's people giving?
- Where do you see God's beauty in creation?

Take pictures with eyes looking for God in the world. Look for where God is already active in the world. Have your pictures developed and bring them with you to next week's session.

Gifts

Can you imagine new ways for people in your congregation to share their gifts in worship? Refer back to the examples on page 117 as a starting point. In your journal, write the names of people or of specific gifts that could be incorporated in the life of worship.

Service

Make a list of ways you live out the gifts that God has given you in the life of worship. What resources have you been given and how do you use them in the life of your local congregation?

'e' ventures

The number of resources for worship available online today is rapidly increasing. Visit www.nooma.com and notice the experiential presentation of the site. Notice how the format of the site frames your visit.

Check out www.sacramentis.com, www.WorshipConnection.com, and www.heartofworship.com as examples of sites that provide a variety of resources for local congregations. For additional worship resources check out the *ReConnecting Woirship* DVD for "Getting Started with Internet Resourcing."

Session Six Video

The video segment on the DVD or VHS in the *ReConnecting Worship Kit* that corresponds to this chapter is Session Six: *Pro-active Co-creators With God*

Chapter Seven
Team Works

She took her place in a row of eight other dancers. Trained in dance from an early age, she was very comfortable in various genres of dance. During her freshman year in high school, she and one other dancer participated in the first creative movement team the church had ever experienced. Now, nine years later, she was standing beside middle- and high-school-age girls who were dancing in worship for the first time. Not only was she dancing alongside these new team members, she was leading the team. A beautiful young woman with a college degree, Kathleen was home for six months before attending graduate school. Though her professional career would take her into international communications, she still loved to participate in the creative movement ministry. Kathleen agreed to work with scheduling, choreography, and encouragement for this growing ministry area while she was home on break. Kathleen's smile and attitude about using abilities to serve God provided the perfect example for these new dancers.

Kathleen grew up in a ministry where teamwork is important. She has always had the ability to work with anyone. Whether others dance above or below her level, she always adapts to the group. She has witnessed many extremes of the word "team," times when the team fell apart and times when the team worked in perfect harmony. Kathleen has seen small teams and large teams. Kathleen has experienced a congregation open to the gift she is able to offer to God. A new generation of dancers enters into ministry led by her humble and encouraging spirit. Through her leadership, another arm of artistic expression was brought to life in worship ministries. Another group of people participates in the creation of liturgy for worship.

If the gifts and abilities of those within the congregation are going to be incorporated into the life of worship, a structure to support this type of participation must be created. Teams form the structure required for this incorporation of resources from within the gathered body. Teamwork is a concept exemplified throughout Scripture. In I Chronicles we see the gifts and abilities of different groups of people used to create the temple. Not only did the people of Israel gave not only of their wealth, but also gave of their time and skill. In Nehemiah, we see a long list of those who contributed to the rebuilding of the wall around Jerusalem. Teams of people from particular areas of the city, as well as family units, are listed as those who took on a particular task in the rebuilding of the wall. The Gospels paint a picture of the way in which Jesus gathered a group of disciples to participate in his earthly ministry. In I Corinthians, Paul wrote of the importance of each individual's contribution to the Body of Christ. Each person's ability and diversity contributes to the working of the holistic nature of the gathered community.

In the Scripture we see the concept of team directly relating to ownership through active participation; a common goal is established and people move forward with purpose. (Acts 2-4) As we look at the purpose of the team, remember what was said in Session Two: "The reason we gather for worship is to celebrate and honor God, to engage and build up the congregation to live out Christian discipleship and to provide hospitable communication that both invites and welcomes others into a fresh experience of and a relationship with the living God."

It would be overwhelming to assign this purpose to one person. Yet in many instances, the preparation and execution of worship is carried out in an individualistic and segmented manner. At times issues of control lead to this pattern. But frequently worship leaders desire more participation in the planning and implementation of worship. The failure to cross into a team-based process can often be attributed to the leader's inability to accept that liturgy is the imaginative and creative work of the people.

Another barrier to the implementation of team-based planning is a misinterpretation of the team role in worship creation. An effective planning team does not sit down and hash out how many choruses of a song will be sung or what type of bread should be baked for communion. Nor do they establish a list of policies and ground rules to control variation. A creative planning team deals with a broader picture of worship. The creative team dreams, imagines, and brainstorms with Scriptures and themes. This creates a multifaceted framework for the stated purpose of worship. The creative team is encouraged to think beyond the way something has been done before and to dream outside of the box. Ideas beyond the realm of possibility will arise, but through the vision of these larger dreams, a more creative reality unfolds.

Leaders often compare this type of creative team to that of a worship committee or guild in some congregations. As you read this material, attempt to put this comparison aside. The word "committee" is not particularly appealing to creative, artistic people. It carries the connotation that rulings will be made and edicts handed down. A creative planning team for worship is concerned with creating *liturgy*, defined as the work of the people, from within the congregation. This team does not meet to make a list of things it dislikes about worship and then engage in lengthy arguments about who is right or wrong. The team evaluates the effectiveness of the creative elements of worship and works in a positive way to provide a worship experience that falls in line with the stated purpose for worship.

To understand more clearly the structure of a creative planning team, we will take a look at several key members of this type of team from both traditional and nontraditional worship models. Though teams will vary in each congregation, some ministry leaders will be members of most creative planning teams.

Team structure

With a variety of worship styles present in today's culture, a creative planning team should represent the individual ministry teams that participate in the creation of worship each week. The number of members of a creative planning team may ebb and flow as ministry areas grow and change. One person might participate in more than one area of worship ministry, bringing a multifaceted mindset to the team. It is important to search for those members who interact with several groups as a worship ministry grows. Too many people participating in the creative planning team process can lead to a choke hold on the process. Though incorporating a diverse group is important, if the group becomes too large subgroups may be necessary to continue the creative process. There also may be ministry area leaders who do not attend the creative planning team meetings on a regular basis but who come to meetings when needed. Starting small and growing into a positive core for each congregation's worship ministry is the best plan of action.

A representative from the welcome ministry and the music ministry could be seen as standard members of this creative team. These ministry areas usually participate in worship on a weekly basis in most congregations. While music might be considered the most obvious ministry area, the importance of a welcome ministry leader might seem odd to some, so let's take a more detailed look at the weekly contribution of the welcome ministry.

The welcome ministry

When a visitor drives into the parking lot, is there an easily accessible parking space available? Is an entryway to the church visible to the visitor? Is there someone to greet visitors when they walk through the door? Is there a detectible pathway to the children and youth areas? Where is the coffee? Where is the worship area? Is a greeter nearby to direct the visitor into the worship area, to make sure the visitor has a bulletin, and to convey any particular information that might be helpful during the worship experience? Are there Welcome Ministry Hosts working to provide for the needs of the visitor?

The Welcome Ministry team is directly responsible for "hospitable communication." The Welcome Ministry Hosts literally open the door for visitors and members alike to experience God. The worship experience begins in the parking lot with Welcome Ministries and flows throughout the service as Welcome Hosts guide, greet, direct, and usher people through the worship experience. The way people are initially received makes a huge difference in their ability to enter into authentic worship.

For those who move from visitor, to regular attendee, and eventually into membership, the presence of the Welcome Ministry team becomes part of the expected atmosphere of hospitality. In turn, members begin to understand that they are to participate in the hospitable atmosphere while on the campus of the church. The Welcome Ministry Host team provides the initial doorway to the worship experience for all attending.

With so much importance placed upon the Welcome Ministry, the leader of this group is a valuable member of the creative planning team. This might be the member who provides the most structure to the group. This person must constantly evaluate the flow and movement of people before, during, and after worship. Becoming a "logistical artist" is necessary for the Welcome Ministry leader. This person must find joy in creatively moving people through the windows of experience that are woven into weekly worship. This person must also evaluate the way in which information and materials are made available to people before and after worship services. An understanding of other activities running concurrently with worship is also necessary for this leader. This person's responsibilities might be considered similar to that of a tour guide, a cruise director, or a flight attendant. "How may I (we) *best* serve you?" is a key element in this individual's planning process.

Including the Welcome Ministry leader in the creative planning team allows for a hospitable atmosphere to permeate the worship experience. This person's sensitivity to the physical needs of visitors and members alike provides the foundation for the rest of a person's experience at church. A hot cup of coffee and a friendly hello may speak more loudly of God's love to someone than the music or sermon ever could. The Welcome Ministry is like thread that holds the pieces of a beautifully crafted quilt together. Without the thread the quilt would be fragments of material, which individually do not possess as much beauty or purpose as when they are woven into one holistic piece.

More teammates

Other members of the creative planning team will be chosen depending upon the gifts and abilities that surface within the congregation. If you have a drama team, an altar team, a group of visual or technological artists, then you might have team members from these groups. You might have a representative from your children's ministry or youth ministry. If you include creative movement or dance during worship then you might include a member of this group on your creative team. Mission and outreach may be a focus that is present in the context of worship, and a representative from this ministry area may contribute to your team. You might have a very creative person who participates in a variety of worship-related ministries, and who brings a big-picture mentality to the creative drawing board. Each church's team will consist of a different combination, but never presume that the people of God in your congregation are lacking in creative gifts to offer through worship. You might begin your team with a pastor, a leader in the music area, and someone who works with the welcoming ministry. Three is a good start, and then you are guaranteed to find more people who are open to God and creativity in worship.

Sometimes it is through the inclusion of a particular artist on the creative planning team that a worship ministry team is formed. You may have a visual artist who is able to contribute art as a way to experience God in worship. This person's creative nature adds great depth to the worship planning process. One week, a piece of art created by this person is used on the altar in connection with the theme of the service and another artist in the congregation becomes aware that there is a place for visual art in the worship experience. This artist in the congregation may never have shared his or her artistic ability if someone else had not modeled it.

The leader and members of the creative team are responsible and accountable to search for those who might be able to live out their giftedness through worship-related ministries. When people join the congregation, is there a print-out made available to key leaders to alert them to the gifts, abilities, and interests of the new members? Is a process in place to contact regular attendees and help them connect with a ministry area within the congregation?

The members of the creative team need to evaluate information received from such assessments in order to seek out those who might find a place in worship ministries. The members of the creative team become those who seek out others to participate in the creation of liturgy for worship. The team members help share the vision with those in their individual ministry areas and facilitate the "work of the people" creatively surfacing in worship.[21]

Leading the creative team

The pastor is generally perceived as the leader of the entire worship ministry, as well as the leader of the creative planning team. The team should see the pastor as one whom God has ordained to leadership, and commit to follow the vision of worship established by the pastor. However, and this is the humbling moment for pastors, even though the pastor's role is guide, it is not necessary that the pastor always be a present member of the creative planning team for worship. In smaller churches, the pastor may be the initial leader of the team. In a larger church setting, or when a pastor serves more than one congregation, a worship director may serve as the leader of such a group.[22] If the congregation has a worship director or someone who functions in the role of coordinating worship, the pastor may choose to have this person facilitate the team. The decision of a pastor to incorporate a creative planning team into the worship-planning process establishes a desirable level of trust. If the pastor trusts the team of creative minds to participate in the planning process, it is not necessary for the pastor to be present during the times these creative minds dream.

Some pastors, music leaders, or church members are concerned about a team-based approach to worship planning for a variety of reasons. (The team might choose the wrong symbols, or lack good taste, and so forth.) When, however, all parties realize the tremendous benefits of a team approach, cooperation and creativity combine to raise worship to a new level. If a person joins the team with the hidden expectation of promoting a particular "worship agenda" or does not support the vision, mission, and ministry of the church, conflict will occur. The ordained leader is then responsible for solving the temporary problem, without falling into the trap of command and control after the problem is solved. Varying ideas and opinions will surface through the creative planning environment. Multiple ideas moving in sync with common direction and purpose create a rich, multifaceted worship experience for the worshiping community.

If the leader is someone other than the pastor (and in many cases it will be), the leader must understand and support the pastor's vision for worship. The pastor and worship team leader must support each other and work together for this type of process to work. If the one set apart to lead the creative worship team does not support the pastoral leadership, thus undermining the planning process of worship, an unhealthy and manipulative structure will form. Both the pastor and the worship team leader must function with open lines of communication. There must be a willingness on the part of both individuals to be flexible. The statement of purpose for worship cannot be set aside to include elements in worship for inclusion's sake. There are times when elements of worship will change at the last minute in order to continue following God's guidance for the service. This may mean removing a piece of music that was rehearsed, changing a visual element that no longer supports the theme of the service, or adjusting a sermon by five minutes. The pastor and the worship leader must have open lines of communication established in order for these changes to be seen as fine tuning and not an attack of personal likes or dislikes toward creative expression.

Whether the pastor or the worship director/coordinator facilitates the creative planning team, several qualities are necessary for the leader of this type of creative planning team.

The leader of the creative team must be an encourager. Working with a creative team requires an understanding of the creative, artistic mind. The diversity of people and their gifts is only intensified when you add the words "creative" and "artistic" to the equation. Writers, dancers, musicians, painters, sculptors, graphic artists—whatever the artistic specialty—can be insecure and temperamental. A leader who encourages each member of the team will greatly reduce these stereotypical artistic tendencies. A worship team leader who is insecure and temperamental will add fuel to any tension and create conflict.

The leader makes it a priority to affirm the gifts of the members of the team. When a person demonstrates giftedness in a particular area, this gift can become normal to those around them. People come to expect great things of that person. Each new creation for an artistic mind begins with a blank page. The questions, "Can I do it again? Can I do better than I did last time? Will this creation be disappointing? What if the inspiration doesn't come? What if no one likes it?" are stirring around in the minds of creative people. Some people do an excellent job of blocking these undermining thoughts. Others need more encouragement and reassurance. As the leader of a creative group, positive affirmation and encouragement become part of the communication with the group as well as the individuals. Insecurity can be greatly reduced by encouragement.

The phrase "temperamental artist" has been applied to many people over time. Bringing an artist into Christian community does not remove the tendency of the artist to be difficult and temperamental. The entire scenario of "temperamental artist" can be avoided most of the time by carefully establishing that the purpose of creativity in the group is not simply for the sake of creation. The creative elements that spring forth from this group are to be used to create a deeper experience of God in worship. The elements are used as tools of creative communication, allowing people more fully to understand their place in God's story. If a song is written, a drama rehearsed, an altar created, or a video edited that does not ultimately meet the needs of the service for which it was prepared, then the artist should not become angered by the decision to cut the creation from a given service. The artist should know that the decision has nothing to do with his or her worth as an artist. The particular element will be saved and might be used at another time. It might be that something prepared needs to be adjusted slightly to work most effectively in the service. In a typical scenario, an artist would find this offensive. However, when preparing art for worship, the artists understand that being asked to make an adjustment is not an attack upon their contribution. It is imperative that the leader of the creative planning team incorporate this thought process as part of the foundational structure of the team. The leader cannot wait for a situation to arise and then try to explain that what has been created will not work in the upcoming worship experience. Establish early the need for each artist to be a flexible team player. It is then the responsibility of each member of the team to establish this attitude in the ministry areas for which they are responsible. If the leader is an encourager and supporter of the artists living out the gifts God has given them, a level of trust and respect will be established.

Another factor that reduces the impact of the temperamental artist syndrome is the emphasis on viewing each team member as a child of God, a brother or sister in Christ. If the team is encouraged to be a group of prayer, care, and support for each other, then the approach to creating dynamic worship as a team will be cast in a new light. If the group encourages and supports one another as friends and family, an entirely different atmosphere is created within the group. Temperamental attitudes are softened by the love and care of Christian community.

The leader of the creative planning team must provide a creative structure and cast a creative vision for team-based planning. Once open lines of communication are established and a team begins to work together, it is time for the leader to provide clear goals and creative vision for the group. The leader of a creative planning team must study the Scripture and thematic flow of the materials communicated by the pastor(s). It is through prayer, reflection, and study that the team leader is allowed to catch a vision for the message God has placed upon the mind and heart of the pastor(s). Whether the style of the pastoral leadership is to follow the lectionary or work thematically through the Christian Year, it is important that the worship director/coordinator spends time connecting with the flow for the upcoming season of worship.

Communicating the Scripture, themes, or series topics for worship services to the team is very important. It is necessary to create printed materials for the team members to use in their own quiet or artistic time. It is the responsibility of the team leader to communicate with the pastors and do preliminary research of resource materials prior to meeting with the creative team. The more information that can be provided to the creative team, the more effective the creative planning time will be.

It is also important for the leader to guide the team in a direction that "harnesses the tension for the purpose of faithful innovation" as discussed in Session Four. Keeping the structure, the theology of the presence and activity of God (the order of salvation), and the hospitable nature for the guest, the stranger, and the sojourner ever-present in the planning processes must come from a continual "re-membering," fostered by the group leader.

The leader of this team must be able to function as an artist as well as an administrator. The group leader must be someone with a creative mind. It might be someone who is gifted in several areas that are incorporated into weekly worship services. This person must be able to visualize how multifaceted elements will merge to produce a holistic worship experience. The leader must be able to incorporate the ideas and requests of the pastor(s) and the planning team, as well as the schedules of all involved. All of this must be evaluated to see what can be accomplished in the amount of time available. The leader must be someone who can set goals, juggle schedules, and meet deadlines in order for the creativity to find its way into worship services. Creative ideas remain only ideas without someone to manage the process. Most who live out the gifts they have been given by God have full-time jobs, responsibilities, and families. It is often the leader who maintains a better sense of what is realistic in the big picture of life. The leader must take into consideration the life of the congregation as well as the lives of the individuals when moving forward with new ideas. This is not to imply that the leader squelch creativity because it sounds like work. The leader must be the one to help others avoid burnout. There is a vast difference between working hard, having fun, and finding joy in the completion of a project, and forcing something that is not attainable, given the time and people available. A leader with an administrative streak can maintain a creative mind while making sure goals are set and follow-through occurs.

Leading a creative planning team can be challenging, yet very exciting. Juggling the ideas and requests of pastoral leadership and artists, as well as the many ideas and requests that come from the congregation, can at times seem overwhelming. The leader of this team must realize that facilitating, training, and deploying people into worship ministry is an artistic genre all its own.

Teams at work to unleash the creativity

With a shared understanding and excitement for team-based ministry established, the work of the team begins. It is difficult to assign the word "work" when describing the activity of creative minds that dream and imagine together in an atmosphere of love and support; "fun" sounds more appropriate. So when this team meets together, make sure a fun environment is part of the process. If providing worship that speaks the language of current culture is important, if being aware of the community in which you live is relevant to the type of worship you provide, if you want to promote a creative atmosphere—then do not meet in a room at the church for your creative planning time! Meet for breakfast or lunch in as many restaurants, coffee houses, bookstores, or malls as you can find in your community. If the local mega-chain has a café, try it out as well. Placing the team in a context beyond the walls of the church enhances the creative process. Remember the song from *Sesame Street*, "Who are the people in your neighborhood?" Who are the people in our neighborhoods? Where do they eat and play? What captures their attention each and every day? How might we more effectively speak the language of those who have never heard the message of God's love and grace? Placing the creative planning team in the midst of culture stretches the creative mind. It also keeps the planning time fresh and new. An ever-changing atmosphere for creative time prevents the group from falling into a slump. Good food and fellowship start the creative juices flowing.

Meeting too often is not healthy for this type of team. Since all of the team members do not determine the weekly details for worship, it is not necessary to have a weekly meeting. However, meeting too infrequently will not keep the bonds of the team strong or carry out its purpose effectively. A once-a-month creative session is a good pattern to establish for the creative planning team. Additional trips or retreats may be added during the year when dreaming further into the future of worship.

In order better to visualize a creative planning session, let's reflect on two different teams' creative planning time.

A rural congregation works on stewardship

First, we will see a small, rural congregation prepare for a yearly stewardship emphasis. There will be four weeks of worship services created around a sermon series entitled, "Living the Gift." The pastor's emphasis will focus on each individual's God-given gifts and how they connect with the larger Body to be the hands and feet of Christ in the world.

The team meets for lunch at a small café in the center of town. The pastor, the choir director, the youth coordinator, and the usher team leader are the core of the planning team. They have invited two others to join them for the meeting: the outreach coordinator for the congregation and the owner of one of the largest farms in the area. The farm owner has no affiliation to a Christian community.

As the meeting begins, the pastor shares the vision for the upcoming series. The pastor explains that this year's stewardship emphasis, a time generally focused on financial giving, will have a more holistic focus. Many people are unaware that giving to God is a way of life, not just placing money in the offering plate. If people can learn to see that living out their own gifts and abilities is part of a life process, then *giving* becomes a natural part of *living*.

The youth coordinator addresses the farm owner before they move further into the planning stage, aware that the farmer is wondering why he was asked to attend. The adult coordinator of youth explains that many within the congregation will be harvesting vegetables soon. For the first weekend of the sermon series, members of the congregation will be asked to bring a portion of their crop to place on the altar. This will give a visual representation of the orally read Old Testament Scripture that describes people giving the first fruits of their crops to God. Second, it will bring the beauty of God's creation into the worship space as a visual reminder of God's provision for humanity. And finally, after the service the food will be distributed to those in the community who are struggling to feed their families. This act will allow the congregation to become part of God's reconciling nature at the point of brokenness and pain in the world.

The pastor requests that the farmer help in the closing of the series on "Living the Gift." The pastor asks the farmer if he might allow members of the congregation, led by the youth group, to glean his fields, once commercial machinery has harvested for the season. The youth group would spend a week picking what the machines had missed. Others in the congregation would help during the evening by preparing the food for storage. The food gathered would be used throughout the winter for a new program that would provide a weekly hot meal for those in need.

The pastor explains that this act of gleaning will allow them to emphasize that God uses all people, even when it may seem one has nothing to give, to be people who participate in the unfolding of God's story in the world. Here again, this will be connected to Old Testament Scripture.

The farmer's sense of relief is evident. Because he was unfamiliar with church life he didn't know if they were going to ask him to donate a tractor, sing a song, or make some type of financial contribution! The creative team's request was one that he could honor. The farmer grants the group permission to glean his fields, thanks them for lunch, and leaves for another meeting in town. The time he spent with the team was quite enlightening for him; he had not experienced a church that was so focused on giving instead of receiving.

The team continues the planning process. Everyone is excited about the farmer's response. They see the project not only as an excellent way to close the series emphasizing stewardship with an outward focus, but also as a positive connection with someone disconnected to Christian community. The team hopes the connection will provide further opportunities to let the farmer know he is welcomed.

The choir director shares with the group several ideas that musically weave the "Living the Gift" theme into the service. One week the children will sing the anthem with the adult choir, reinforcing the concept that each person of every generation has a gift to be lived each and every day. One week a simple song will be shared that has been written by someone in the congregation in response to the series theme.

Next, the outreach coordinator informs the planning team that she has been in contact with children's Sunday school teacher(s), and they create colorful cards of love and encouragement to accompany the food bags to be delivered. Plans to include an information/sign-up card in the bulletin for those interested in helping with the new hot meal program are also made. Now that the gleaning has been approved, she will continue to coordinate those who will help with the project.

As the team finishes the meeting, they brainstorm other ideas for the series. They discuss the importance of the financial part of the sermon series. The focus of living out all of the gifts given by God is not to diminish the need for monetary commitment to the church. The team agrees that the prayer for this particular time in the life of the congregation is that people will gain a greater awareness of what they have been given and what they have to give. The hope is that the congregation will more fully understand that working together with what God has given each individual makes a difference in knowing and sharing the love and grace of Jesus Christ.

An urban congregation plans for Easter.

The second team plans an Easter service and the weeks to follow. The Easter service, entitled "Breaking the Seal," will end one sermon series that focused on "breakthroughs" and begin a new sermon series following Easter entitled "Life as a Work of Art." The pastor does not attend this team's meetings. Instead, a worship director or coordinator for the congregation leads the meeting.

The restaurant of choice for the day has a long saltwater fish tank down the middle, with a large mirror on one side to give depth to a small space. The lunch crowd pours in. The restaurant is located at a very busy intersection of a large city. The server pulls tables together for the group near the requested electrical plug for the laptop. The leader carves out a workspace at the end of the table for materials. The server is warned in advance that the group might stay a while.

The Scripture for Easter is not surprising; it is the story of the resurrection. "Breaking the Seal" refers to God's power over death through Jesus' death and resurrection. Scripture from Exodus 14 will be included, reflecting upon the Israelites deliverance from Pharaoh. The sermon portion of the service will encourage people to look beyond past failures, sins, and successes and see into the future offered by God. The sermon will move toward the question, "What is your greatest work of art?" The answer: "It is the next one." The challenge and sending forth for the congregation will be to look to the new future God is creating in each person. Regardless of the past, God's activity in the world calls us to participate in an exciting new way.

The creative planning team is very excited about the new series that will begin. However, time is first spent reviewing the worship experiences since the last creative planning time. How has worship affected each team member? What has been especially meaningful for each individual in the last month? What elements of worship have caused others to draw closer to God? Have there been verbal responses from other church members? Have there been any issues concerning the flow of the service that need to be discussed?

After a time of reflection, discussion of the upcoming services begins. Over the past year the team has been searching for the right moment to create an outdoor "congregational mosaic" during a worship weekend. A church member mentioned to the pastor that a local merchant will provide the molds for mosaic picnic tables. These tables would go perfectly in the church's new prayer garden, where picnic tables are needed. A team member agrees to explore the costs and possibilities of this type of activity. People will be given a piece of the mosaic during the service and place this piece into the mold as they leave worship. This will be an engaging activity that will be inclusive of all generations.

The attention turns to the children's participation in the Easter service. Can the children, many visiting with parents in worship for the first time, be sent home with something tangible that reminds them of God's love and creativity for their lives? Further discussion sparks the idea of a pack that will be created for each child to receive during children's time. The kit will contain crayons and a bookmark of the risen Christ that they may color during worship and take home.

The conversation then turns to a discussion of live artists painting during the Easter worship services. The pastor requested that the two artists paint during the service, completing the work as the closing music ends. After a few minutes of discussion about the possibilities and logistics, it is discovered that several youth are very artistically gifted and might be able to serve as artists for the service. Through the course of the conversation, a multigenerational list is established.

A clarification of service times is discussed, since an extra service will be necessary for the Easter weekend. Logistical issues in regard to time and space are considered. With the initial theme for Easter established, individual team members now have information with which to dream during the upcoming weeks. Special music, drama, graphics, clips, visuals, or other creative ideas will surface after time is given to reflect on and think about the theme and Scripture.

The team then moves on to the weeks following Easter. The inclusion of other artists during worship such as potters, woodcarvers, and quilters is discussed. A reminder that confirmation weekend will fall in the "Life as a Work of Art" series sparks another discussion. An early artistic idea for the children for Easter is now being moved to the confirmation weekend. In the pastor's sermon, the story of the ostrich egg hanging in the Temple in Jerusalem will be shared. Ostriches have really big eyes but not much brainpower. If they do not keep one eye focused on their egg while roaming in the desert, the egg will be lost. The people of Jerusalem have an ostrich egg hanging in the temple to remind them to always remain focused on Christ while engaging in the activities of the world today.[23] For the weekend of confirmation, the altar ministry will incorporate beautifully decorated ostrich eggs designed by the confirmation class. The confirmands will hear of this tradition while away on confirmation retreat and spend time decorating the eggs as they reflect on the call to keep Christ first in their own lives. This will re-emphasize the story, it will provide each confirmand an opportunity to participate in the creation of worship for his or her service of confirmation. Each child will have a beautiful, tangible memory of this important time of study and preparation. After a discussion of the best deals on purchasing ostrich eggs (ostrichesonline.com) in bulk and the appropriate paint to use, the team turns to closing comments regarding the upcoming weekly service.

What you do not see in the details described above is the prayer, laughter, and fellowship that occurs during the seventy-five-minute planning sessions of these two groups. You do not hear the wild and zany ideas that do not make it to the service. You do not see the interaction of the team with other patrons in the restaurant. You do not hear the leader's encouragement of each person to share "life" with one another, the prayer requests mentioned, or a report from a previous prayer heard. You do not hear requests or needs of individuals voiced and the answers to the requests met immediately from within the group. With all of these things woven into the planning time, it is really family time between fellow artists. God uses this time in a multilayered way. Big picture ideas, smaller details, and meaningful moments are created around the table of food and fellowship in Christian community. Ideas and dreams that, over time, have produced hours of authentic worship experiences as well as the momentum to include hundreds of people in the creation of liturgy for worship, have come forth from the creative planning table. At the same table a small group full of love and support, spilling into the various areas of ministries represented, is formed.

Navigating team process

Every congregation finds itself in a different situation when approaching change in worship planning and implementation. It may be that a congregation is a new church with great enthusiasm for authentic worship and is building on a fresh foundation, much like those who built the new temple in I Chronicles. The excitement and support of the people are centered in a common desire to reach out in a whole new way with the message of God's love.

It may be that a congregation more closely identifies with the rebuilding of the wall in Nehemiah. Times of transition and change may have caused a sense of breakdown in what was once vibrant worship; the congregation chooses to work together to build a new structure upon an existing foundation. At times, this process is slow and painful, yet new life can still emerge. The congregation sees the signs of new life as a revival of a rich and powerful heritage.

Whatever scenario a congregation most closely resembles, Jesus' model of team-based ministry frames the context for the convergence of tradition and innovation. As a new covenant emerged, the time and energy Jesus spent with his disciples prepared them for ministry. They became actively involved in sharing the message of Christ with others. They took ownership of God's love and grace, and their purpose became that of proclamation to the world. The disciples' excitement led to other people's participation in the knowing and sharing of the gospel message. This "team" faced joy and pain together. They questioned and doubted at times. Jesus' presence did not remove the disciples' humanity. In the same way, team-based worship planning allows people to take ownership, set goals, and move forward with purpose—a purpose that allows the gospel message to be passed on to new generations. With Paul's reminder in I Corinthians of each individual's unique contribution, the diversity in the team becomes a point of celebration. There will be times of joy and pain, as well as questions and doubts. Human tendencies will be present, but with Christ as the center of the team, authentic, engaging worship will result.

Who are those within your congregation that might serve as a core for a creative planning team for worship? Is there someone sitting in your worship service each week with a gift that might add an element of creative communication to your worship experience? Who might help organize a team of people to bring forth the "work of the people" within your own congregation? How might this type of planning help reach beyond the walls of your congregation in a way that connects the message of the gospel with those who have yet to find their place in God's story?

Chapter Seven Connections

Prayer, Presence, Gifts, Service

This week you will incorporate *Prayer, Presence, Gifts, and Service* into one activity. In preparation for next week's session pray about and begin to brainstorm ideas around the following Scriptures. Think about resources that might help effectively convey the message.

Planting

As you reflect upon these Scriptures, imagine who might be present at your first month of worship experiences. What types of imagery or other methods of communication might be most effective in communicating the gospel to them?

Mark 8:22-25

They came to Bethsaida. Some people brought a blind man to him and begged him to touch him. He took the blind man by the hand and led him out of the village; and when he had put saliva on his eyes and laid his hands on him, he asked him, "Can you see anything?" And the man looked up and said, "I can see people, but they look like trees, walking." Then Jesus laid his hands on his eyes again; and he looked intently and his sight was restored, and he saw everything clearly.

Music:

Art:

Poetry:

Movement:

Images:

Prayers:

Other:

Philippians 4:13
I can do all things through him (Christ) who strengthens me.

Music:

Art:

Poetry:

Movement:

Images:

Prayers:

Other:

'e' ventures

Websites to enhance the creation of weekly worship services are increasing. Willow Creek pioneered this type of planning tool. Check out Willow Creek's "Build Your Service" option at www.willowcreek.com. Also, visit www.WorshipConnection.com for another service-building search tool. Use these websites to contribute to your *Prayer, Presence, Gifts, and Service* activity this week. Remember to look for pieces or ideas from each site. When acquiring elements from a variety of sources you will locate materials that you cannot use or do not particularly recognize as theologically fitting; this is okay. Search with a positive attitude and take time to look for things that might work in your particular situation. A resource that is inappropriate for your situation may be perfect for someone else. Over time you will identify particular sites that are more aligned with your particular needs. However, a broad "search scope" attitude will keep you abreast of the variety of resources available. What other websites can you locate to enhance the planning process?

Session Seven Video

The video segment on the DVD or VHS in the *ReConnecting Worship Kit* that corresponds to this chapter is Session Seven: *In a Resource State of Mind.*

Chapter Eight
In the Worship Kitchen

Mona Lisa Smile is a movie set in the 1950s. Julia Roberts plays the part of art history professor Katherine Watson, who moves from the West Coast to take a job as a professor at Welsley College. Her hope is to touch the minds of the brightest women in the nation and inspire them to see and pursue opportunities in life beyond the horizons of current expectations and roles. In one of her classes, she describes and displays van Gogh's *Sunflowers* and invites the students to reflect on his technique as she tells them it was not appreciated during his life. She tells her students that he never sold a painting, but after his death, as people realized the genius in his work, he became famous and his paintings skyrocketed in value. While the students think about the risk and creative investment in van Gogh's artistry, Katherine brings out a paint-by-number kit of the same painting. They read the words on the box, "Now everyone can be a van Gogh. It's Easy." As the students look at the contrast between the risky creativity and the easy paint-by-numbers art-in-a-box, they are struck by the irony. True art is not easy. It requires work, patience, commitment, and a willingness to risk. The same thing is true of worship design. Worship is not paint by numbers. It, too, is not easy. It requires work, patience, creativity, and a willingness to risk.

Perhaps holding up van Gogh as an example of the creativity required for the worship planner is a bit intimidating. After all, how many of us would imagine that we are capable of that level of skill or creativity? Another image, however, might be helpful in understanding the process of worship design and the role of the leaders: cooking. Everyone must eat. In this section we explore the worship planning and design process by looking at two culinary activities: *meal planning* and *cooking gumbo*.

Meal planning

Let's explore a model for putting into practice what we have been learning by looking at worship planning for an entire year.

I worked with developmentally disabled adults while I was in seminary. I had a job as a follow-along counselor. My task was to assist my clients in their efforts to move from institutional life into life in the community. There were times when I served as advocate in the work-place. Sometimes I was a sounding board for on-the-job frustrations. Sometimes I helped those who were sharing an apartment become more effective in their interpersonal communication. One of the most com-mon tasks I helped with was something that most people (or at least, most men) don't really think much about: meal planning.

Once each week we would sit down with a meal-planning form and discuss who would be cooking what night, and what they could make that would be both nourishing and edible. We reviewed the contents of the refrigerator and the pantry to see what they had on hand. We exam-ined the budget. We spent a considerable amount of time discerning what resources they would need to create the meals, and how they might have a balance of familiarity and variety in their diet. Then it was off to the gro-cery store—each with a part of the list to find what they could, sometimes asking for help or directions, sometimes improvising a little, and some-times finding a surprise that they could include in a particular meal. Occasionally one of them would get a windfall, like frozen casseroles from parents, or fresh veggies from the garden at the home from which they had graduated. One would even receive an annual shipment of frozen salmon from his father. The process was fascinating because the planning could not be taken for granted. Each of them always wanted to advocate for his or her favorite dish, or suggest going out to eat.

This process took patience and planning well in advance. Resources, skills, and timing all had to be considered. The alternative would have been to go to the store, buy whatever looked good at the time, and then for each of them to come home and grab whatever looked good. Without patience, planning and guidance, they would have lived on potato chips, Twinkies, popcorn, peanut butter, and tamales from a jar. Sadly this hap-pens as well in the homes of many busy or stressed out families.

Even though I have assisted people with meal planning, I still strug-gle with the task at times myself. Many times I come home at supper-time and my wife, my son, and I ask each other, "What do you want to do for dinner?" Then begins the familiar ritual, almost as if it were a new experience each time, yet with the same results. We look in the pantry, stand in front of the refrigerator with the door open, or gaze into the foggy freezer thinking, "We should have gotten *that* out this morn-ing. If we had gotten *that* out, we could have had it for supper." By this time, hunger becomes more pronounced, homework calls, and there is still the entire evening ritual of baths and so on. Almost without fail, we decide that one of us will run out and pick something up at a fast food place. We settle for unhealthy fast food because we failed to plan.

Now, it's not that I don't like to cook. I love to prepare and serve creative and healthy meals. I like variety and experimentation, as well as some of the old standard comfort-food recipes that have been handed down from generation to generation. Yet, because of our over-full schedules, this lack of planning repeats itself. Over time I have come to two very important conclusions: *You can't cook what you don't have*, and *it doesn't work well to microwave a frozen turkey*. Cooking takes planning, preparation, access to the right resources, and patience. The same is true of worship.

How often have I heard worship planners say, "I wish I had thought of that sooner; I know a song that would have been perfect in that service." Or, "If only I had had more time, I could have done this or that really creative thing." The culinary rule applies to worship: "You can't cook what you don't have" and "you can't microwave a frozen turkey." Worship as the creative and purposeful work of the Body of Christ, like meal preparation, requires planning well in advance. It requires an awareness of available resources, a budget, a familiarity with sources for various special needs, a prayerful sensitivity to the needs of the congregation, and a willingness to spend time listening to God's direction.

Over time I have developed a longer-range model for worship planning that, much like "dinner-planning-for-a-week" when I was a counselor, allows us to be prepared in advance. We have developed a process of "worship-planning-for-a-year." Of course we can't plan for every eventuality. No one knows when there will be a tragedy or a cause for a special celebration. Congregational life, like family life, remains flexible and somewhat light on its feet. But for the most part, we have found that it is easier to develop meaningful worship if we have the right resources (can't cook what you don't have). If there is something we want to do that requires extra time, we know that we must "thaw and leave time for roasting."

People have asked me if all this planning hampers the creativity and spontaneity of the Spirit. Most of the time (depending on who is asking) I tell them the story of the preacher who was busy doing "this and that" all week and didn't make time to prepare his sermon. He thought to himself, "The Spirit will inspire me with the right words at the right time." Sure enough, as it always does, Sunday morning rolled around again and when he got up to preach, he closed his eyes and asked the Spirit to give him the words. Indeed the Spirit did speak. The Spirit said, "You should have prepared." Planning is not chiseled in stone. We see it as a work in process, and we always want to adapt if necessary and move when the Spirit actually says "move."

We work in thematic series loosely based on the Christian year and modified by the particular rhythms of our congregation and community. This model would work as well for both small and large churches that follow the lectionary, or even with some adaptation for those who organize worship in other ways, such as around themes or metaphors. The key is to lay out the structure for the year and to begin projecting and imagining.

Some of the elements of the rhythms of the year and the specific needs of the congregation and community are:

- *The Christian year*—The major themes in the life of Christ are set in an annual cycle in the form of a rhythmic pattern. This pattern allows the church to experience the breadth of the gospel story in the course of each year. The themes follow a two-year (Anglican or Catholic) or three-year cycle (most Protestants).
- *Specific congregational emphases*—Particular facets of a congregation's life or goals find expression in the themes and focus of worship, whether they are preparing to construct new facilities, emphasizing a new mission project, engaging in an intentional outreach program, or encouraging the congregation to participate in new educational programs or a network of small groups.
- *Rites of passage* are woven into the fabric of congregational development. Confirmation, graduation, or sending students off to school all provide opportunities for members of the congregation to share in the celebration and the affirmation of these important life events.
- *Motivating the congregation* toward deeper involvement and discipleship can also shape the content of the worship services. Recruitment for different areas of service and ministry and developing financial stewardship are two examples of such motivational emphases.
- *Growth in knowledge and love* is an overall goal of worship. Pastors and worship planners must understand the needs of the congregation and develop worship themes and sermons that contribute to building up and edifying the congregation in these areas.
- *Foundations of faith* are an important area to include in an annual worship planning process. It is good to remind the congregation annually of the basic foundations of what it means to participate as a member of the Body of Christ. This emphasis is important for longtime members as well as newcomers to the faith. Focusing

specifically on the foundations of faith and community serves to instruct those who are new to the congregation, reminds existing members of the nature of their commitments, and allows visitors to overhear expectations of membership and learn what it is that membership might mean for them. It is also good to emphasize the foundational memories and purpose of each particular congregation. These shared purposes and memories build congregational cohesion and focus energy.

While some of these facets of congregational life and planning may vary from year to year and from church to church, we have found that if we plan for these, we keep the congregation growing spiritually and numerically as it flows with the rhythms of worship.

The main blocks of time that we plan during the year are:

• Advent and Christmas

In many ways, Christmas has become more of a cultural phenomenon than an activity of faith. This cultural dynamic has a great effect on the understanding of the season for members of the community. The season of Advent is an important time for emphasizing the themes of expectation and preparation as well as offering one alternative to the extreme pull of the materialistic celebration.

• The New Year

Our associate pastor is from Tonga, where the celebration of the New Year is a major emphasis. They hold revivals and special worship services, including a watch night service. Their celebration of the New Year is one of the major festivals of the year in the church. We combine this energy with the model Adam Hamilton uses at the Church of the Resurrection for launching new series when more people are present to hear. He looks for issues or themes that will draw the interest of those visitors who attend only on Christmas Eve and on Easter and announces a new series that will begin the following Sunday. While they are present and attentive, the invitational dimension of the Great Commission is activated. The idea seems to work well, and it certainly counters the traditionally low attendance patterns that the church typically experiences in the weeks immediately following major holidays.

• Lent

Lent is a season to focus on spiritual growth and introspection. Frequently we develop a series of worship services that invites the congregation to examine the inner life and the quality of relationship with

God. This season is also an excellent time to encourage the formation of short-term small groups to encourage accountability in the process of reflection. Planning in advance allows for the development of study materials that help groups focus on the content of the worship experiences as they pray together and encourage one another.

Palm Sunday is developed as a service involving the participation of several groups in the congregation. We encourage participation in Palm Sunday because this becomes the entry point into the experience of the Holy Week Journey. The Maundy Thursday/Good Friday service(s) are also important times to involve members of the congregation in the telling of the story because it encourages active participation in and a deeper understanding of the events that lead to Easter. The experience of the Easter celebration is deepened by intentionally involving as many members of the congregation as possible in the events of the preceding week.

- Easter

This festival celebrates the resurrection and is a high point of the Christian Year. It is also one of the greatest opportunities for the proclamation of the gospel to people who attend church infrequently. Special care is given to the planning of this service; we include elements of language and images that are familiar to those outside the Christian community, even as we remain faithful to the traditional celebration of the events.

- Post-Easter Series

While many churches consider the week following Easter a "low" time, we try to launch a series of services that will attract people who visited on Easter weekend and who might return the following week. If we assume low attendance and plan accordingly, we have unintentionally disappointed those who might have been inspired on Easter to return and "give it another try." If they come one weekend and are moved by excellent worship and overwhelming congregational excitement, and are moved to return the next weekend only to find everyone taking the week off, they might wonder, "If everyone was really so excited about Jesus and the power of the resurrection, why aren't they here this weekend? Was it just a show? Was it a bait and switch?" This experience can unintentionally train "Christmas and Easter Christians" to remain in that pattern.

- Pentecost

Pentecost commemorates the birth of the Church. Frequently we combine our celebration of Pentecost with the Confirmation of the young people who make a commitment to join the church. This occasion serves as a wonderful opportunity to recount the power of God's Spirit at the birth of the church, the purpose and passion of the people on the day of Pentecost, and to connect that experience to the lives of those being confirmed as the same purpose, passion and spiritual birth is shared.

- Summer Series

We live in a community that experiences transience and movement during the summer. Many people move to the area during the summer, and as they move to a new community, they search for a new church home. Many members of the congregation, because of vacations, camps, and college breaks, are transient. During summer, we try to provide continuity that will keep the regular attendees involved in learning and growing, but we also seek to make each service stand on its own. Because of the increased number of visitors, we develop services that are welcoming and inviting for newcomers and provide themes that engage regular attendees and encourage continuity of participation. Some of the series we have held during the summer have focused on the parables of Jesus, the miracles of Jesus, pathways to spirituality, and the promises of the Bible.

- Back to School

This time has a pronounced rhythm in our community, with an affect that is similar to a New Year event (which is in part the legacy of an agricultural society that brings in the harvest). People in our community focus on restoring a schedule and making a new beginning. The focus during this season is usually practical and designed to attract people who might want to find direction in life. Our goal is to help people in the congregation refocus priorities.

- Stewardship and Thanksgiving

Fall is traditionally harvest time, which is the reason a focus on stewardship traditionally was placed during this season. We are not in a farming community, but we have found that as we move toward Thanksgiving and the close of the Christian year, the rhythm of giving back to God fits well here.

The rhythms of the church year, as well as the patterns and needs of the community, provide the worship planner with a framework for shaping worship that will attract, edify, and encourage members and visitors. What are the particular rhythms of your congregation's worship life? What are the rhythms of your community? When do you experience new visitors? How do you design worship to mesh with and enhance participation according to these natural rhythms?

The right spice

Our associate pastor and I work together to imagine, anticipate, envision, plan, and prepare for the upcoming year. We have found that we work better with someone with whom we can pray, read and discuss Scripture, share ideas, check for sanity, and keep the other focused on the process. In the initial phases of planning for the seasons of the year, we gather information about the needs and the particular congregational emphases for the coming year. We attempt to look into the future in order to anticipate the needs of the congregation and the patterns of the community. We gather resources for study and inspiration. We spend time reading Scripture and praying about the members of the congregation, as well as those who are outside the church. As we project into the future and consider both those inside and outside the church, ideas begin to emerge that serve to guide us in the worship-planning process.

Retreat

A planning retreat is critical to the long-range model of worship design. We carve out two or three days away from the office and away from most distractions. We do what we can to make sure that the needs of the church are covered and we remain available in case of absolute emergency. As we think rhythmically, thematically, pastorally, and pedagogically about the needs of the congregation and community, we pray and read Scripture. Of course we don't accomplish a year's worth of planning in two or three days, but it is surprising how much we accomplish.

The most helpful tool to assist us in this process is the creation of a file on the computer with the date of each weekend service listed. The dates are separated by the themes and milestones of the Christian year and by the major emphases of the congregation. This document is a work in progress that provides an outline upon which to hang ideas, stories, and creative possibilities for worship as we think of them. Before I used this method, I was always coming up with good ideas, writing them on a piece of paper or the back of a legal pad, and then misplacing and forgetting about them until the perfect opportunity to use the idea had passed. You may have seen the pieces of string art woven on hoops called dream catchers. Our document, which is always nearby in my laptop, serves as an idea, story, creativity, and inspiration catcher. By the end of the retreat, we come away with a loose framework for the entire year, several ideas for specific series, and sometimes even several outlines for sermons and ideas for worship.

Tuesdays with Sione

The other crucial dimension of the planning process is the day I spend each week in planning, prayer, preparation, and writing. Most Tuesdays I spend the day with our associate pastor. (He is really more like *my* pastor.) We focus on the particulars of upcoming sermons and worship services. Some ordained ministers might think, "It must be nice to have an associate pastor with which to plan and a staff to watch the church while you are out." 1) Yes it is nice, although it hasn't always been this way. When I started at this church I didn't have an associate pastor; in fact, I didn't even have a congregation. 2) I worked with this plan for several years before we did have an associate pastor, or a director of worship. For several years I met with another pastor and friend. We decided that we could work with the same overarching annual framework and tweak our sermons and our thematic emphases according to our individual congregation's situation and needs. It worked well. Even when he was serving a much more formal congregation, we still found great benefit in planning together. The sermons and the expressions of worship were different, but we shared the framework, the fertile ground of prayer and sharing ideas, and we kept each other focused on listening to God and stretched out into the future. This process could be adapted to work with a pastor and a lay leader with knowledge of the Bible, a good sensitivity toward the needs of the congregation, and an interest in and commitment to excellence in worship.

Our time together captures emerging ideas and develops a foundation upon which to build scriptural teaching and worship experiences that will encourage, comfort, challenge, center, and send the congregation, as well as welcoming and involving new people who will come. Sometimes we develop ideas with great intent. Sometimes the opportunities that emerge surprise us.

As Sione and I were discussing the Advent season for the upcoming year, we discovered that both of our fathers were coming into town prior to Christmas. We laughed about the "wise men from afar," but the more we thought about it the more we realized that their presence might be something that would be a blessing for the congregation, as well as a fresh experience of an old, old story. We decided to invite each of them to preach one weekend in Advent. My father has served as a pastor and as a seminary professor for more than fifty years. His experience and wisdom brought new perspective to the congregation and allowed them to see a picture of continuity, and a living multigenerational witness to the gospel. Sione's father has served churches in Tonga for years. He has been a church planter, a pastor, and a District Superintendent. Because his father does not speak English, Sione needed to translate for him. The choir from a Tongan church in Dallas came to worship and shared with us that weekend. This was a rich and meaningful moment for the congregation and a powerful window into the reality of the global nature of the gospel message. On Christmas Eve, our families served communion together. Across cultures and generations, the gospel message was shared in living witness. This idea, as well as the time and effort needed to coordinate and develop all the elements of this experience, would not have been possible without our time on Tuesdays. Our time together allows creative ideas to emerge.

Following our annual planning retreat, we meet with the Director of Worship Ministries to share ideas and to receive feedback. The information we provide is not complete. Sometimes it is a guiding image, sometimes a story, sometimes a list of Scriptures. We want worship design to be a shared activity. After our meeting, the Director outlines the information and brings it to the creative ministry team for further reflection and development. If a congregation does not have a worship director, the pastor or other planner could share this material with a group of other creative individuals who might include the choir director, the altar guild, or the worship committee. After the team reflects on the information provided and brainstorms resources and ideas, we meet again and develop clearer outlines for the coming seasons of worship. While this process may seem intimidating, the benefits are well worth the effort. Ideas have time to germinate. There is a high degree of ownership and involvement, and the cross fertilization of ideas provides for a deep expression of worship that is truly the work of the people.

Cooking gumbo

Emeril Legasse is a phenomenon across the country. His excitement about cooking, the way he engages an audience with his ability to entertain, his gifts for cooking, and the experience of the food that is prepared draws people to attend his shows, buy cookbooks, purchase his cooking supplies and spices, and fill his restaurants all around the country. My son and I love to watch him cook. Something about his passion, inspiration, and creativity keeps us coming back. One of my favorite dishes that I have watched Emeril prepare is gumbo. If you are not familiar with gumbo, it is a type of soup or stew that can be made with a variety of ingredients. In

New Orleans, the most famous type of gumbo is seafood. There is nothing like a big, cast-iron pot filled with a rich gumbo, made with fresh crabs, shrimp, oysters, crawfish tails, and sausage. It is fun to cook and it tastes wonderful. It makes for a great meal for lots of people and most of the time (the way I cook it—following the model of my mother's cooking proportions and hospitable attitude) there is plenty to share.

Why am I telling you about gumbo? In the process of making gumbo, we can find some illumination for the creation of worship as the service of the people of God.

The chef depends on four things: 1) a recipe; 2) the cooking methods that he or she has learned from previous cooking instructors, culinary experts, or family members; 3) a knowledge of where to obtain the right ingredients; 4) his or her taste buds. (No matter how closely one follows the recipe, if the gumbo doesn't taste good, something needs to be changed.)

Gumbo begins with a roux. The roux is a paste made with flour and butter. It is heated slowly and browned in the heavy cast-iron pot. The roux is the substance that blends all the flavors, thickens the gumbo, and binds ingredients together. Without the roux, the gumbo would be just a thin soup.

Essential to each of the different gumbo recipes is the combination of bell pepper, onion, and celery. Emeril calls this simple vegetable combination "the trinity." These three vegetables are chopped, sautéed, and stirred into the roux as the foundational flavor base. No matter what type of gumbo is going to be made, the trinity is always there as the foundational flavor. Because they are added so early in the cooking process, they usually break down and become invisible and individually indistinguishable. But just because they are not seen doesn't mean they are unimportant. If any one of these three ingredients is missing, the gumbo doesn't taste right. It isn't balanced.

According to what ingredients are available to the chef, a number of different ingredients can be added to the recipe, yielding very different results. There may be chicken and sausage, or shrimp, or crab and oysters, all of which make excellent gumbo. You might end up with a gumbo made primarily with shrimp and a rich Creole tomato flavor, or a gumbo of chicken, sausage, and okra. What holds the gumbo together (roux) and the foundation of flavor (trinity) are always the same, but the available ingredients give each recipe its individuality.

As the ingredients are added and simmered gently, the flavors converge into a new reality that nourishes and delights. Right before it is served, some freshly chopped green onions are stirred in. Sometimes there is extra cayenne pepper, Tabasco sauce, or filé (ground sassafras) to "kick it up a notch." These things are frequently added at the table because people's tastes and tolerance for spice vary widely.

It may sound strange, but cooking gumbo shares many similarities with designing faithful and effective worship.

The worship designer depends on four things: 1) *Scripture*, the recipe; 2) *tradition*, the processes and information passed on by those who have gone before; 3) *reason*, the use of the mind to analyze, interpret and locate resources appropriate to the task; and 4) *experience*, the sense of what works and what does not when worship is implemented. (If the congregation or the community rejects it, something may need to be changed.)

Begin with a roux—This is the combination of prayerful preparation and patience. If you rush the roux, it doesn't turn that chocolate brown color that contains the smoky flavor base. Likewise, without prayerful preparation and patience, worship design will lack depth and cohesion.

The foundation is always the Trinity—Just as the foundation of the gumbo is always Emeril's "trinity" (onion, green pepper and celery), the foundation of Christian worship must assume and acknowledge the presence and nature of the Holy Trinity—Creator, Redeemer, and Sustainer. This means that the nature of the life of the worshiping community is to be in the image of the triune God. As we seek to develop worship experiences, we use the Trinitarian identity as a model. Worship is creative and redemptive. The purpose and the person of Jesus Christ shape worship. Worship is inspired by the Holy Spirit and is a channel for the Spirit's continued inspiration. Someone shared with me a phrase found on the bottom of a worship bulletin: "This is the tentative order of worship—the Holy Spirit will determine the actual Order of Worship." There is always room for movement.

The ingredients available determine the individual character and flavor of the worship. Worship is made up of the individual gifts and contributions of each particular congregation. These gifts combine according to the communication styles, cultural realities, and particular needs and setting of the community. Worship, like gumbo, requires the interaction of many members: tradition, innovations, and the gifts of the congregation. A variety of liturgies and forms can be shared across cultures and locations, but worship develops as unique to the community in each particular situation. According to the makeup of each congregation and community, each church will have some diversity in its expression of worship.

Sometimes when traveling I suggest that we stop to get something to eat, and usually, with the acute sense of radar, my son will locate a McDonald's. My wife and I, however, like to eat at restaurants that are not generic. We like little places that have a regional feel. We can get to know something about the people through the food that is served. Frequently we find ourselves on the horns of this dilemma. The issues surrounding worship at the intersection of tradition and innovation. have many similarities with that dilemma. Some people want familiarity and would rather experience the same thing on a regular basis. Others prefer creativity, individuality, and change. This challenge faces congregations and worship planners all over the world. Is there only one type of food that should be served with a standardized and changeless menu, or is there room for regional cuisine and adaptability? Pedrito U. Maynard-Ried tells us, "The great experiment in North American liturgical circles is how to make worship a truly multicultural experience."[24]

Increasing numbers of people find their cultural identity in a postmodern multiculturalism more than they do in what is considered to be traditional Euro-American culture. These people are being touched by the power of the message of the gospel and bring their own forms of expression into new and existing communities of faith. Christian members of the postmodern culture bring new expressions of music and a great familiarity and expertise with technology as a form of both communication and artistic expression.

Even McDonald's, with a menu that has been relatively stable throughout decades of existence, has changed and adapted what it offers in order to meet the changes in the surrounding community. New information about health risks associated with a high fat diet led the menu planners to "lighten up" the menu offerings. The changing tastes of the aging Baby Boomers also caused the chain to make important adaptations in the food. Like the burger chain, churches are faced with similar choices.

Look at the following examples of three churches facing the changes taking place in the world around them. See how the courage to involve the resources, language, learning styles, and music affected the congregational life and health. Two of the churches chose creativity and change guided by purpose and tradition; one of them chose not to change.

Church One

On the southern coast of England in the seaside city of Brighton, there is a large tabernacle built by a congregation that was born during the revivals connected to the ministries of George Whitfield and John Wesley. The tabernacle is a large and impressive building in a prominent section of the city. The building is in good repair and is filled most days of the week by people from multiple generations. Laughter and music can be heard from the street. Originally it was designed to accommodate large gatherings of people filling the main floor and the balcony of the sanctuary. In many ways the tabernacle is the same as it has been for a couple of centuries; in some important ways, however, it has changed dramatically. The tabernacle no longer houses a congregation. It is now a bar and restaurant. It feels strange to look around the place and see a bar where the chancel rail used to be. The area that once housed the organ pipes now holds liquor bottles and large televisions showing NASCAR races. On the walls in the half dome above the chancel are painted images of Jimmy Hendrix, Tom Petty, and John Lennon. Painted above the dome are the Latin words that render, "drink yourself to death."

I asked around to find out what had happened to the old congregation and was told that all of the members were aging and dying. The congregation made no effort to understand and reach those who surrounded the church. As a result, no new people joined the church, even though the population in the area was increasing. Eventually, the small congregation could not support the facility or its mission any longer, so they decided to sell it to the developer, who changed it into a bar.

Church Two

Across the street from Christ Church College in Oxford, England, is another old church. I was told that this church dates back to the 1100s. As I walked past the old building, I noticed that many of the gravestones in the front of the yard were toppled and broken. A temporary chain link fence surrounded the graveyard. I imagined another church declining into inactivity. Something posted on the temporary fence caught my eye. Laminated and mounted on the chain link were pictures painted by children. The pictures also contained words— God is love, God is creator, God is good, God is giving, God is forgiving, and many more. I rounded the corner to see what was happening inside. I found the door locked, but there was a note posted on the door that said, Wednesday night worship: 6 P.M. Curious, I decided to return later.

I arrived at about 5:45 and approached the building. A very old gentleman welcomed me and handed me a bulletin. I walked into the ancient sanctuary and saw rows and rows of chairs arranged in a semi-circular pattern facing the side of the sanctuary (rather than the distant and elevated chancel area at the end). People of all ages gathered and talked throughout the sanctuary.

The room quickly filled and the music began. The congregation began to sing passionately a combination of ancient hymns and current worship songs. There was no large screen above the platform to block the beautiful ancient stained glass through which the evening sun filtered dramatically. Instead, video monitors were mounted on the huge marble pillars scattered throughout the room, painted to match the marble. They didn't seem out of place at all, but strangely brought a sense of holy relevance in the midst of the formal worship area. We sang for several minutes, read psalms, and prayed. The visiting minister delivered a powerful sermon, during which members of the congregation followed him in their Bibles as he moved from passage to passage. Toward the conclusion of the service, the pastor invited the congregation to pray, and then to respond to various invitations. People were invited to come forward if they wanted to discover more about entering into a relationship with Jesus. Another invitation was issued for people to come forward for prayer for healing, direction, comfort, and encouragement. One final invitation was given for people who wanted to share stories of what God was doing in their lives with some church leaders and pastors in a different area of the chancel. I watched as people poured forward. While they gathered in front of us, the rest of the congregation continued to sing. As I sang, I looked down and noticed that my shirt was wet. Tears were streaming from my eyes, because I had seen the rebirth of hope and the activity of God in a church that had been in a severe pattern of decline. This vision gave me a hope for the church itself and is part of the reason I am so passionate about the subject of worship and helping congregations wrestle with its importance.

Church Three

While visiting Ulsan, Korea as a leader at a conference on worship and multimedia, I was moved by the faithfulness of the congregation hosting the event. This was a congregation that was willing to take risks. When we arrived, we were met with deeply traditional Korean hospitality. We were welcomed warmly and treated with dignity and respect. As we made our way into the sanctuary, we found it filled with ministers and lay people of different ages from all over the country. They had come great distances to participate in this experience of worship and learning.

The majority of the church in Korea is very traditional in its expression of worship and is growing rapidly. However, several ministers have noted that there are large segments of the population who are not attracted to traditional churches. Korea, like many Western nations, is experiencing the effect of generations who have grown up, tremendously influenced by technology and various forms of electronic media. As they thought and prayed about how to communicate the gospel with this most rapidly growing segment of the population, they decided to try some different ingredients in the creation of their worship services. They wanted to keep the recipe the same, but they decided to create the services with a different flavor and style.

The pastor and worship planners began to develop worship experiences using electronic media to enhance communication and to engage the people in the experience of worship. A large projection screen dropped down from the ceiling on cue in the front of the sanctuary and was used for the projection of lyrics and images that enhanced the message of the songs. At times, moving video was layered behind the text to invoke deeper understanding and to touch the heart, mind, and soul of the people. The sermons were biblical and called for response and commitment on the part of the congregation. The music blended traditional hymnody with modern instrumentation, and the style of the music varied from rhythmic world music to the more classical and meditative.

One of the most moving experiences occurred when a college dance group entered the liturgy. They were dressed in a variety of costumes ranging from high tech to ancient biblical. The dramatic dance unfolded with precision and energy as the dancers acted out scenes depicting the struggles of modern life. Woven throughout the performance was the activity of the dancer who represented Christ. As he moved among the various scenes of pain and brokenness, he brought restoration and hope to the other dancers. Toward the end of the modern dance, a powerful ancient scene depicted the suffering, death, and resurrection of Christ. Without words, the dancers captured the hearts and minds of the congregation and communicated clearly the age-old message of the redemptive power of Christ in the world. I was even more impressed when I discovered that many of these dancers had come from a life outside the church, deeply involved with the drug culture and other destructive situations. This church had developed a style of worship that shaped the community, used the gifts of many of the members, and attracted large numbers of people, young and old, to share in the service, the story, and the experience. It was living out the call to create a community of storydwellers and storytellers. (That gumbo was different from any I had experienced before, but was it good? Oh, yes!)

These churches exist in far-off places, but I could name church after church in the United States and around the world in which one of these three scenarios is being played out. Not all of the churches that adapt to the needs of the congregation and community are moving toward the high tech. Many are moving into what Leonard Sweet calls the "ancient future," a term that means the creative appropriation of the practices of historical and ancient Christianity, combined with more contemporary methodologies. The two churches above not only survive but also continue to thrive. They used the recipe of Scripture, tradition, reason, and experience; the roux of prayerful preparation; ingredients of the communication styles and gifts of the congregation and community; and services balanced and flavored by the Trinity. In situation after situation this recipe enables the creation of faithful, innovative, and authentic worship. The resulting gumbo of worship was different in style and flavor, but the content, purpose, and outcome were the same.

Take a moment to reread the descriptions of the worship services described above and jot down things you notice in response to the following questions. These reflections will be part of our discussion in the following session.

- What elements were used to adapt to surrounding culture?
- How was the purpose of the church served?
- What elements of tradition were maintained?

Now reflect on your worship service(s).

How has your church adapted, or how does your church need to adapt, to surrounding cultural changes, in order to fulfill the purpose of worshiping God?

How do we make certain that services are engaging, excellent, and meaningful for the congregation and those who would come as guests, visitors, and potential members?

Blessing for a meal

During our time together we have learned that this is not really a question about the "right" or "wrong" ways to worship. *The real issue pertains to accepting people who are different than we are when we meet God.*

Sione, the associate pastor at Grace Community UMC, wears a tupenu. A tupenu is part of the Tongan formal attire for men. It is a skirt that is wrapped at the top by a wide cummerbund-type belt, made from woven reeds or braided leather. As you might imagine, the tupanu is not something that is a normal part of the traditional male fashion scene in Shreveport, Louisiana. I am happy to say, however, that Sione is accepted, loved, and respected in the congregation. When his father came from Tonga to Grace and preached in Tongan, with Sione translating, two of the men in the congregation (not Tongan men) wore tupenus as a sign of respect and to show support, accept-ance, and welcome. My son also has one now and wears it occasionally. Sione's cultural background is different. His dress is different. His accent is different. His preaching style is different. But the style, content, and outcome are faith-ful to the message, purpose, and direction of the gospel. Some communities would not have accepted him because they are more comfortable with the familiar and resistant to change. I am thankful that this congregation was accepting. He has brought a great deal of perspective, a deep focus on spiritu-ality and prayer, and has influenced the life of the congregation greatly. If we had not been accepting, we would have missed those gifts.

In the Book of Acts we read Peter's account of his strange vision that led to Cornelius's conversion, and the sharing of the gospel with the Gentiles. In the Scripture, Peter is sharing with some of the circumcised believers who are upset with him for having gone to eat with and share with an uncircumcised man.

> I was in the city of Joppa praying, and in a trance I saw a vision. There was something like a large sheet coming down from heaven, being lowered by its four corners; and it came close to me. As I looked at it closely I saw four-footed animals, beasts of prey, rep-tiles, and birds of the air. I also heard a voice saying to me, "Get up, Peter; kill and eat." But I replied, "By no means, Lord; for nothing profane or unclean has ever entered my mouth." But a second time the voice answered from heaven, "What God has made clean, you must not call profane." (Acts 11:5-9)

This is a strange-sounding text. The man has a vision of a sheet filled with all kinds of animals landing on the ground before him, and he hears God telling him to eat them. Peter refuses to eat, because, according to all he has been taught and all he has experienced, these animals are unclean and thus off limits. But God says, "What God has made clean, you must not call profane." It is a powerful message that paved the way for conversion—not only the conversion of Cornelius, the Gentile with whom Peter shared the gospel, but also the conversion of Peter himself. Peter was committed to living a life of faithfulness to God and to Christ. He knew the rules in the Scripture about what kind of people and food he was supposed to avoid. He wanted to be careful to guard and keep the traditions that had guided his family and his people, but God expanded his horizons and lifted him into a new and larger reality. The convergence of tradition and innovation is vitally dependent on the principal of Peter's vision, response, and conversion. God taught him not to react to things that were different, but to be open to the surprising movement of the Spirit as new generations of worshipers encounter God. In a sense, what is required from us is a willingness to allow ourselves to be open to the possibility of being constantly converted. We encourage you to pray for that attitude of openness and to exercise it as you consider the implications of *ReConnecting Worship* in your congregation.

Chapter Eight Connections

Prayer

Pray for each person in your *ReConnecting Worship* study group. Pray for the time you will spend together in your closing session. Pray for the discussion of how your group can participate in new and creative ideas for worship.

Presence

Reflect upon your participation in the *ReConnecting Worship* study. How have you been encouraged during this process? How have you been challenged? How have you been excited by the possibilities for innovation in worship? Take a few moments to write down specific ideas or questions you might have as you think about the future of worship in your congregation.

Planting

As the worship-planning process begins for your congregation, how will you insure that appropriate time and space given to the priority to worship development? How can you support the pastor in the planning process and maintain accountability for this support?

Gifts and Service

Obtain the ingredient you were assigned to bring with you to the closing session. Regardless of how large or small your item may seem, it is an important part of the recipe!

'e' ventures

As you prepare for an evening in the kitchen with your group, visit the following links and explore some of the interesting ways that people use available resources to make unique gumbo creations. Imagine the diversity of worship throughout the church as you explore. http://www.gumbopages.com/food/soups/gumbo-de-savoy.html and http://www.recipesource.com/main-dishes/seafood/octopus/alaska-gumbo1.html www.emeril.com.

Session Eight Video

The video segment on the DVD or VHS in the *ReConnecting Worship Kit* that corresponds to this chapter is Session Eight: *Working Together.*

Leader's Guide
Managing the Group Experience

Session One

Before the first session, read the "A Broken Chalice," which is the introduction to *ReConnecting Worship* and review the video segment to be shown during class.

Supply List:
✓ TV and DVD or VCR
✓ Dry erase board or easel pad and markers
✓ A *ReConnecting Worship* book for each participant
✓ A blank journal or notepad for each participant

Welcome participants. Express your excitement that they are accompanying you on this nine-week journey.

Describe what participants can expect:
1. Begin with prayer.
2. Participate in group activity and discussion.
3. View video segments.
4. Read each chapter in the book and complete the *Prayer, Presence, Gifts, and Service* worksheets or exercises during the week.

Distribute *ReConnecting Worship* books and journals to participants.

Discussion: Ask the group these questions:
❖ What brings you here today?
❖ What do you hope to learn from this study? How do you expect to grow?
❖ What is your role in worship as you begin this group process? (i.e., Are you a worship participant, a leader, a planning member, etc.?)

Ask persons to be committed for participation.
Say: This study is helpful for individual growth, but its effect will be most important for the congregation as a whole if we agree to participate

together, making every effort to do the reading and *Prayer, Presence, Gifts, and Service* sections, as well as attending all of the sessions unless you are ill or have an emergency.

Read Prayer of Preparation: Have participants turn to page 14 and read together the prayer as printed.

Show Video on DVD or VHS (length: 13 minutes)
Session One: Finding Common Ground and Renaming the Problem

Discussion: Ask the group the questions below. Take notes on the group's responses on the dry erase/easel pad while directing the group turn to page 28 in the workbook and take notes in the *Prayer* section. This discussion will guide the *Prayer* portion of the activity during the upcoming week. *(Be sure to copy your notes in your participant's book at the end of class.)*
- ❖ Who makes up your congregation?
- ❖ Can you identify those "weeping" at change?
- ❖ Can you identify those "rejoicing" at change?
- ❖ Can you identify points of tension within your congregation?
- ❖ Can you identify points of tension within the group in which you are participating?
- ❖ Who makes up your surrounding community? (i.e. saltwater swimmers)

Discuss the upcoming reading assignment for the week.

Review the *Prayer, Presence, Gifts, and Service* activities that are to be completed by the next session.

Go forth in peace.

Session Two

Supply List:
✓ TV and DVD or VCR
✓ Dry erase board or easel pad and markers

Open with prayer.

Discuss last week's *Presence* activity. Ask each person to explain a childhood memory and explain how it affects his or her worship experience in the present day. As the leader, begin by explaining your item of remembrance.

Discussion: Ask each person to share his or her response to the "Your Church" activity on page 25 in the workbook. Ask someone to take notes on the dry erase board/easel pad on the group's response to the church's *Identity*, *Situation*, and *Worship* style.

Ask:
❖ What is positive about the responses?
❖ What might be considered negative about these responses?

Show Video on DVD or VHS (length = 17 minutes)
Session Two: Mission, Tension, and the Great Commission

Ask:
❖ What motivated the church to start a new service?
❖ What steps were crucial in forming support within the congregation?
❖ What were some of the outcomes once the service proved to be "successful?"
❖ What thoughts came to each of you individually as you listened to this church's story while processing your own situation?
❖ How does viewing a new service as a "mission," an opportunity to reach out to those who have never been exposed to a faith community or the grace of Christ, modify your perspective of new forms of worship?

Discuss the upcoming reading assignment for the week.

Review the *Prayer, Presence, Gifts, and Service* activities that are to be completed by the next session.

Go forth in peace.

Session Three

Supply List:
✓ TV and DVD or VCR
✓ Dry erase board or easel pad and markers
Open with prayer.

Discuss last week's *Gifts* activity. Have each person explain his or her worship timeline as they draw it on the dry erase/easel pad. Alert the group to take note of similarities and differences as each person's history is shared and discuss.

Discuss last week's *Presence* activity with the group. Have someone take notes on the dry erase board/easel pad as to the responses received from each group member.

Ask:
❖ What similarities are found between generations?
❖ What responses are unique to a particular age group?

Show Video on DVD or VHS (length: 12 minutes)
Session Three: Cultural Archaeology and Emerging Worship.

Discuss the upcoming reading assignment for the week.

Review the *Prayer, Presence, Gifts, and Service* activities that are to be completed by the next session.

Go forth in peace.

Session Four

Supply List:
✓ **TV and DVD or VCR**
✓ **Dry erase board or easel pad and markers**
✓ **A current church bulletin for each participant**

Open with prayer.

Discuss the artifacts found during this week's *Presence* activity. Encourage each member to explain the "story" the artifact tells and why it is meaningful.

Show Video on DVD or VHS (length: 8 minutes)
Session Four: Change Happens! Do We React or Do We Respond?

Discussion: Ask the group the questions below. Delegate someone to take notes on the group's responses using the dry erase/easel pad. The responses should include physical items as well as cultural experiences.
❖ What has been a normal part of your life experience that was not part of your parents' or grandparents' life experience?
❖ What will be a normal part of the life of emerging generations that has not been a normal part of your life experience?
❖ How do the responses of the first two questions affect the way people connect with worship today?

Distribute the bulletins to each participant.

Discuss the upcoming reading assignment for the week.

Review the *Prayer, Presence, Gifts, and Service* activities that are to be completed by the next session.

Go forth in peace.

Session Five

Supply List:
- ✓ TV and DVD or VCR
- ✓ Dry erase board or easel pad and markers

Open with prayer.

Discuss this week's *Presence* activity. Encourage each member to express his or her response to the experience as well as explain the significance of the item of remembrance acquired.

Show Video on DVD or VHS (length: 12 minutes)
Session Five: One Generation Shall Tell Another . . .

Discussion: Ask the group the questions below in response to the story of Jonathan as seen on the video. Have someone take notes on the group's responses using the dry erases/easel pad.
- ❖ How was Jonathan with people?
- ❖ How did he learn the story?
- ❖ How did he share in telling the story?
- ❖ How was he received in hospitable communication?
- ❖ How did he enter a shared sacred space?

Discuss the upcoming reading assignment for the week.

Review the *Prayer, Presence, Gifts, and Service* activities that are to be completed by the next session.

Go forth in peace.

Session Six

Supply List:
- ✓ TV and DVD or VCR
- ✓ Dry erase board or easel pad and markers
- ✓ A disposable camera for each participant

Open with prayer.

Discuss this week's *Presence* activity. Ask the group to answer the questions below. Ask someone to take notes on the group's responses by using the dry erase/easel pad.

❖ What was positive about your experience as a visitor?

❖ What might have been more helpful for you as a visitor?

❖ How can you as an individual become more active in creating a hospitable atmosphere during the weekly worship experience?

Discussion: Ask the group to respond to the *Remember and Proclaim* section in last week's reading (p 95 of the book). Ask someone to take notes on the group's responses using the dry erase/easel pad.

Show Video on DVD or VHS (length: 10 minutes)
Session Six: Pro-active Co-creators with God

Discussion: After reading about the 9/11 service in last week's Chapter Five, as well as viewing pieces of the service in today's session, ask the group the questions below in response to the service.

❖ How was *Service* encouraged or demonstrated?

❖ How was *Love* conveyed?

❖ How were participants encouraged to *Remember* and *Proclaim*?

❖ How were participants encouraged to *Go forth*?

❖ How were participants encouraged to *Live*?

Distribute the cameras to each participant.

Discuss the upcoming reading assignment for the week.

Review the *Prayer, Presence, Gifts, and Service* activities that are to be completed by the next session.

Go forth in peace.

Session Seven

Supply List:

✓ TV and DVD or VCR

✓ Dry erase board or easel pad and markers

Open with prayer.

Discuss this week's *Presence* activity. Ask the group to explain how they "saw God" in one or two of the pictures taken over the past week. Encourage each individual to reflect upon his or her response to this type of activity.

Show Video on DVD or VHS (length: 9 minutes)
Session Seven: In a Resource State of Mind

Discussion: Ask the group to brainstorm each of the topics below, keeping in mind that you are doing so with "worship eyes." Ask someone to take notes on the group's responses by using the dry erase/easel pad. As the leader, share some examples to stimulate the flow of creative thinking. Use the following questions, as mentioned in the video, to guide your activity:

❖ What are the material resources available to you?
❖ What are the gifts of the people that might be shared in your community?
❖ Try to imagine at least one new way that you could share God's story.

Use the following topics for brainstorming. *Remember: materials and ideas do not always have spectacle or special effects. Creative thinking outside the box will help you find what might best express God's story.*

❖ Love   ❖ When life isn't fair
❖ Forgiveness   ❖ Our changing neighborhood
❖ Questioning   ❖ Giving
❖ Anger

Discuss the upcoming reading assignment for the week.

Review the *Prayer, Presence, Gifts, and Service* activities that are to be completed by the next session.

Go forth in peace.

Session Eight: In the Worship Kitchen
Supply List:
✓ TV and DVD or VCR
✓ Dry erase board or easel pad and markers
✓ Copies of the *Group Planning Sheet* found on page 141.
✓ A recipe for the gumbo or soup you will prepare as a group in session nine. Suggested recipes can be found on page 162.

Open with prayer.

Show Video on DVD or VHS (length: 3 minutes)
Session Eight: Working Together

Distribute a copy of the planning sheet to each participant.

Discussion: Ask the group to begin the planning session as explained in the video segment based on the information gathered from last week's *Prayer, Presence, Gifts, and Service*. As the leader, decide how the group will divide into teams. An effective tactic is to separate into teams of two or three for planning a service around one of the Scriptures listed. If the group involves no more than three, choose one of the Scriptures for planning.

Ask the group to consider the target congregation to be planned for. Will the group plan a service that is targeted to a multigenerational congregation, a particular age congregation, or a service that is targeted to a particular perspective (i.e. aquarium dwellers, aquarium visitors, saltwater swimmers)? If you have multiple groups, consider assigning different target congregations to each group. For instance, one group might use the passage from Mark 8:22-25 for targeting a multigenerational congregation while another group might use the same Scripture to design a service that targets saltwater swimmers, in other words, those unfamiliar with church language and culture. Decide what will be most effective for the needs and local setting of your group.

Allow each small group to explain to the larger group the flow of the service and the elements to be used.

Decide as a group the location of the next session. If you are conducting this study at your church, you may want to request the use of the kitchen for your next meeting. Or, you may decide the home of a group member would be more conducive to the closing session. You will need to meet in a location that has access to a TV and VCR/DVD as well as a kitchen large enough to allow the entire group to participate in the preparation of the meal.

Assign each person an ingredient from the gumbo or soup recipe you will use. Also, decide who will bring supporting items you might wish to have as a group such as bread or crackers, tea, dessert, as well as any plates, napkins, cooking utensils, etc. Encourage the group to use the *Gifts* and *Service* section in the upcoming week's chapter to make note of the items they will be responsible for.

The group leader is advised to keep a comprehensive list of what is decided and send a reminder note to each participant in the group in the next few days regarding the special closing session. Create the reminder letter in an "invitation" style, as if you were inviting each member to a party. Include direction as to the time and location as well as a reminder of the item(s) each person is to bring.

Remind the group to read the final chapter and complete the *Prayer, Presence, Gifts, and Service* section.

Go forth in peace.

Session Nine: In the Worship Kitchen

Supply List:

✓ TV and DVD or VCR

✓ The recipe for the gumbo or soup you will prepare

✓ The items of each member of the group

Open with prayer.

Show Video on DVD or VHS (length: 9 minutes)
Session Nine: More Together Than Alone

Prepare the chosen recipe as a group. Have fun! As you prepare the recipe, reflect as a group on the three churches described in the weekly reading and consider any implications for your own church from what you have read.

Gather together around the table and give thanks for the beautiful creation you have prepared. As you share in this meal, have group members reflect upon the process of this study. Ask the question: How has this study deepened your understanding of worship? How has this process changed the way you view the creation of worship? What are ways that you can take what you have experienced and share it with your worshiping community?

Say: This is the closing session of this series, but we anticipate that it will not be the end of our discussion of the important challenges and opportunities facing our church. What "next steps" might be appropriate for us to consider as individuals and as a group as we support the worship ministry of our congregation?

Close in prayer.

Notes

[1] James Russell Lowell, "Once to Every Man and Nation," *The Book of Hymns* (Nashville: The United Methodist Publishing House, 1966), p. 242.

[2] Merriam-Webster Online. http://www.merriam-webster.com.

[3] "Affluenza" (PBS, 1997).

[4] Stanley Hauerwas and William Willimon, *Resident Aliens* (Nashville: Abingdon Press, 1989), pp. 139-140.

[5] Donald Miller, *Reinventing American Protestantism* (Berkley: University of California Press, 1997), 17. These statistics are based on Gallup polling data. However, Kirk Hadaway and other sociologists who actually count heads have demonstrated that church attendance is half of what Gallup reports: 20-25 percent of the population on any given Sunday.

[6] The primary sources of the information in this section: Pedrito U. Maynard-Reid, *Diverse Worship* (Downers Grove, Ill: InterVarsity Press, 2000), and Robert Webber, *Rediscovering the Missing Jewel* (Peabody, Mass: Hendrickson Press, 1997).

[7] Thomas G. Long, *Beyond the Worship Wars* (Herndon, Va: Alban Institute, 2001), p. 13.

[8] Webber, *Jewel*, p. 114.

[9] Marva J. Dawn, *Reaching Out Without Dumbing Down* (Grand Rapids, Mich: William B. Eerdmans Publishing Company, 1995), p. 93.

[10] Daniel T. Benedict and Craig Kennet Miller, *Contemporary Worship for the 21st Century: Worship or Evangelism?* (Nashville: Discipleship Resources, 1994), p. 122.

[11] Miller, *Reinventing*, p. 3.

[12] Dawn, *Dumbing Down*, p. 93.

[13] Theodore R. Weber, *Politics in the Order of Salvation* (Nashville: Abingdon Press, 2001), pp 409-410.

[14] Marcia McFee, *The Worship Workshop* (Nashville: Abingdon Press, 2002), p. 17.

[15] Townley, *Designing Worship Teams*, pp. 130-131.

[16] This section is adapted from an article previously published as "Spontaneous Liturgy," *Leader in the Church School Today*, Fall 2002, p. 3. Used with permission.

[17] Redman, Robb, *The Great Worship Awakening: Singing a New Song in the Postmodern Church* (John Wiley & Sons, Inc. Jossey-Bass, 2002), p. 208.

[18] French folk-tale.

[19] Wheatley, Margaret J., Turning to One Another Simple Conversations to Restore Hope to the Future (Berrett-Koehler Publishers, Inc. © 2002 by Margaret Wheatley), pp. 78, 79.

[20] Handt Hanson, *Mission Driven Worship: Helping Your Changing Church Celebrate God,* Changing Church Forum (Loveland, Colo.: Group Publishing, 2001), p. 13.

[21] The resource, *ReKindling Your Music Ministry*, which is included with this book in the *ReConnecting Worship Kit*, uses a music ministry's structure and process to demonstrate a team model for individual ministry areas. Additional copies can be obtained at your bookstore for the music leaders in your congregation.

[22] In nineteenth and twentieth-century structures, when a pastor served more than one church, often the Sunday school superintendent was the chief leader in the church and even planned worship prior to the church school, when the pastor was away. In the twenty-first century, given rapid changes in worship over the past decade, consideration should be given to designating a worship director for the role of team leader, especially when the ordained minister is traveling a circuit.

[23] Adapted from Leonard Sevet's Sermon at Grace Community Church, February 2004.

[24] Pedrito Maynard-Ried, *Diverse Worship: African American, Caribbean, and Hispanic Perspectives* (Downers Grove, Ill: Intervarsity Press, 2000), p. 46.